Published by Semiotext(e)
2007 Wilshire Blvd., Suite 427, Los Angeles, CA 90057
www.semiotexte.com

Versions of some of these essays were originally published in *May revue*, *Artforum*, *Reality Sandwich*, *Moyra Davey—Speaker Receiver* (Sternberg Press), *The Long Century*, *Spike Magazine* and *Stefan Brüggemann* (JRP Ringier). Grateful acknowledgment to the editors of these publications.

Thanks to Robert Dewhurst and Sarah Wang.

Inside cover photograph: Janet Kim
Design: Hedi El Kholti

ISBN: 978-1-58435-098-9
Distributed by The MIT Press, Cambridge, Mass.
and London, England
Printed in the United States of America

10 9 8 7 6 5 4

Chris Kraus

# Where Art Belongs

semiotext(e)
intervention
series □ 8

# Contents

# 1. No More Utopias

1

YOU ARE INVITED TO BE THE LAST

TINY CREATURE

**1.**

*Tiny Creatures is not a gallery. It is Tiny
Creatures.
Tiny Creatures is not a venue. It is Tiny
Creatures.*

— Janet Kim, Tiny Creatures Manifesto 2007

In the winter or spring or maybe the summer—
depending on who and when you ask—of 2006, Janet
Kim moved into the storefront at 628 N. Alvarado
that would become Tiny Creatures. Divided into two
rooms, the store was one of six offices in a new-ish low-
rise cement structure about 20 yards north of the spot
where four access ramps to the 101 freeway meet
Alvarado. Located at the arterial edge of Echo Park
near downtown LA, the storefront's immediate neighbors were a bootleg trailer, an ice truck, a vacant lot,
and a ramshackle house occupied by an old woman

who lived alone with her dog. The 1000 square foot space had a toilet, a shower, and a full kitchen. "It was exactly what I was looking for," Kim remembers. Suffice to say, there was hardly any pedestrian traffic. The American Apparel at the corner of Alvarado and Sunset had yet to be built. The boutique and café littered strip of Sunset Blvd. that ends at the foot of the downtown Los Angeles skyline was still a collection of 99 cent stores. When Tiny Creatures took off and hundreds of people gathered outside the storefront at openings, she remembers collecting the beer cans and giving them to the old woman next door to cash in as recyclables. At the time of this writing (summer, 2010) the building appears to be vacant except for Transportes Mendez in #630, a truck-parcel business that serves Guatemala.

In any event, Tiny Creatures was born at the height of the Bush years: sometime after Abu Ghraib, after the arrest of Buffalo artist Steve Kurtz on terrorism charges, but most likely before the preemptive detention of the Muslim doctor in Boca Raton who was finally charged in a "plot to treat wounded terrorists." These external occurrences poisoned the atmosphere but on an immediate cognitive level; they mattered less to Kim and her friends than the concurrent real estate boom that was transforming low-rent Echo Park—a haven for generations of immigrant families, artists and writers—into LA's hottest new neighborhood. As Matt Fishbeck would later recall:

"This [was] in Echo Park, which used to be cheap and very bohemian but these days is so tony that— no lie—half of our friends are homeless and the other half are terrified. In a climate of unorthodox and uncertain living—you gotta be prepared to be displaced and learn to live that way. I won't lie—it's chaos, and I love it." ("We Have Tiny Creatures for Neighbors," *Fake/Real* Issue #4.)

The rent was $1100—a stretch; Kim used her credit card—and her general plan was to build a back room to live in and use the front as a space to share with her friends. She and her boyfriend Ben White were already founding a new indie label called Tiny Creatures to record and distribute the music made by the LA underground bands who were their friends. But while the start date of the lease remains hazy, Kim is certain that Tiny Creatures began as a gallery on September 16, 2006 with an exhibit of collages and drawings by musician/artist Ariel Pink and writer/artist/musician Andrew Arduini. A lot gets lost in the chaos of a creatively amateur enterprise where the people in charge are artists themselves—and in their mid-to-late 20s, trying to juggle the demands of running a space that is at heart altruistic with their own art and careers and the panic-drenched unspoken question hanging above everyone's head—*Where Is This Going?*

But Kim is an excellent archivist. Looking at the hundreds of photos she keeps in her old desktop PC, I see ladders and beer kegs and girls in black tights and t-shirted guys taping stuff to the wall. A timeless bohemia. They're more or less the same photos I saw when we were preparing the book about David Wojnarowicz and his friends/collaborators in the East Village '80s… the same photos preserved in hundreds of libraries all over the world documenting artistic experiments of the last half century. As Hedi El Kholti, one of the later participants at Tiny Creatures wrote, "other misspent youths long gone, who made proclamations, lived in yet-to-be-gentrified neighborhoods, took drugs, started record labels, made art… *My life to live*. Later on these artists could be rediscovered… or then again, not… Is this supposed to be part of the narrative?" (*By The Time You Read This I'll Be Gone*, 2009).

The history (forgotten or not) of Tiny Creatures is recent and most of its participants are still here. While I never frequented the gallery—being mostly out of LA during its short, vivid life span—I'm aware of its legacy reaching beyond its participants to the life of the city. Kim's inspired improvisation as the founder/creative director of Tiny Creatures played a pivotal role in transforming the Los Angeles art world from a cluster of fiefdoms ruled by a handful of MFA programs into something more urban and open. Knowing little of the insider discourse around visual art or the medieval mentality that defined the art game in LA, Janet Kim changed it.

Janet Kim is a willowy 28-year-old woman with almost waist-length dark hair whose tentative presence and soft speaking voice belie both her determination and her post-punk vocal performances that have been variously described as "sweet," "gorgeous and dream-like," "enveloping," "dark," and "bloodcurdling howls blurring the lines between pain and pleasure."

We meet several times at the house in the back of a bungalow court in the Angelino Heights district of Echo Park that she shares with her new partner, Garrett Cathey. They met at an art-show/house party in Canyon Lake, a Lake Elsinore suburb in eastern Riverside County. Kim was back home helping to care for her father during the last months of his life; someone gave her a flyer outside the local mall Borders. Garrett, 24, a collagist and poet, was living in a small town near Hemet, and working as an industrial painter, via various other points in California five years after finishing high school. At the end of one of these visits, Kim gives me a copy of *Found and Lost*, the 'zine made by Cathey's best friend and roommate Michael De Witt during those days. *Found and Lost* features obscure collages and poems by late-Parisian surrealists Mary Beach and Claude Pelieu. I met Beach and Pelieu towards the end of their lives nearly three decades ago in New York; at the time, they were living on Beach's small income five hours away in rural Cooperstown, occasionally driving into the city to meet up with old friends and attend art shows and readings. As I leaf through the 'zine I'm struck with the thrill of transmission. How did the work of Beach and Pelieu—largely forgotten in their own lifetimes—manage to reach a lone writer living near Hemet without a BA outside of any institutional orbit?

In an essay El Kholti wrote to mark Tiny Creatures' last show (by then, things had fallen apart due to perennial causes), he remarked:

*What I find compelling about the scene at Tiny Creatures is that although discerning in her tastes, Janet Kim brings a generosity and sincerity to her curatorial adventures. The place becomes at once a music school, a screening room, a performance space, an art gallery... but mostly it's a fragile proposition. I suspect that part of that may come from the fact that, like me, she comes to this culture from the outside. What she likes is not a given, or self-evident. When you're an outsider, Culture retains an element of strangeness. It's a learning process, you have to make it yours, and this brings an element of surprise to your choices.*

When I explain to Janet at our first meeting I'd like to record the history of Tiny Creatures, she takes this quite literally. She's been laying low since the recent death of her father, but she'll try and think back. She'll open the archive.

Born to Korean immigrant parents, Janet Kim began playing piano when she was four. Her father, who'd been a teacher by day and a jazz musician by night in Seoul, worked as an auto mechanic in East LA. As Kim's childhood progressed her practice-time escalated to more than four hours a day. By the time she was 8, her father had saved enough money to open his own shop in South Central and the family moved to Montebello, where they became active in the Young Nak Presbyterian Korean church: congregation, 8000. "I grew up in the church," Kim remembers. "I started a gospel band when I was 13"—the songs, as arranged by Kim, sounded a lot like U2—"and the spirits came in after that. My grandmother was a shaman. As a child, I was taught to be a psychic and the church seemed to encompass the belief of what I knew of the world."

On track for a career as a classical soloist, Kim received a scholarship to Northwestern's Conservatory Program. During her four years in Chicago she played keyboards in bands. She began to question the path she had chosen in high school, and also the church. "The church was so huge. It seemed like the whole world—that's how the world was. It was like being part of a cult. It was hard to get out of." But finally when she traveled to China during her third year of college, everything changed. "There was a huge shift. I was finally completely liberated."

After traveling in the US and living briefly in New York, Kim returned to Montebello in 2002 with a music BA and no idea what to do. The church and her old world seemed strange and distant; she could no longer relate to its most basic precepts. Body to blood? "I couldn't connect to it." Also, she noticed that all the church members aspired to a completely assimilated middle class lifestyle. "They could not understand why you would not want to be that. Or want anything else." She pauses and puffs on a $1.50 cheroot. "That past still haunts me. But for me, the church was really always about love. And I can still take that with me."

Teaching piano and working part-time as a coffee shop waitress in Montebello, she felt completely alone. She was recording her own music on keyboards in her old childhood room, but she knew she had to meet other musicians. Looking for people she might connect with, she began coming into the city to listen to music.

In 2005 she rented a room in Echo Park and met Ben White, the founder of Part Time Punks, a popular club night held at The Echo, a bar on Sunset where people who'd grown up as misfits with obscure musical tastes danced for the first time outside their bedrooms. Part Time Punks provided a much needed venue for the city's new underground bands. For the next several years, White would be Kim's boyfriend, bandmate, and partner. In LA, she met other musicians like Matt Fishbeck, Ariel Pink, Rachel Detroit, and Geneva Jacuzzi.

Fishbeck recalls meeting Kim at a post-Christmas party she and White hosted. "It was that time right after Christmas when everyone's come back from their families to whatever hovel they're living in. I saw the piano and I remember thinking, *Who lives here?* Ben told me she also played drums. Holy Shit needed a drummer. I asked her, *Are you any good?* And she said, *Yeah, I'm pretty good.* By the end of the night she was the new Holy Shit drummer." After her long exile in Montebello, the energy of Echo Park's still very local punk underground scene wasn't lost on her. Everyone was playing in each other's bands: Jacuzzi's Bubonic Plague, Pink's Haunted Graffiti, Fishbeck's Holy Shit. Between 2005 and 2007 when she and White started her band Soft-boiled Eggies, Kim, Pink, and Fishbeck comprised the Holy Shit line-up.

As she remembers, "At that time a lot of people started coming together at places like The Smell [a no-alcohol underage venue] and it just solidified into a group of underground bands. Not everyone liked each other, but it was a great place for musicians to meet." So when Kim signed the lease on 628 N. Alvarado sometime in 2006, it was with the idea that the space would be somehow communal. Tiny Creatures had already released Ariel Pink's EP *My Molly.*

Kim can't remember exactly when the plan changed and Tiny Creatures, the musician's hangout and studio, became Tiny Creatures, the gallery. Although she hadn't studied visual art, during her early years in LA she developed an interest in architecture: reading Italo Calvino and Mike Davis, visiting Sci Arc studios "just to see what the architecture students were doing." She began going to galleries, watching art movies, and becoming aware of the art used on record covers. Still, none of her close friends at the time were in art school (Pink had attended CalArts' MFA studio program in the early 90s but his and everyone's primary focus then was on music). But she *thinks* she got the idea on the night—or was it the nights?—when she, Fishbeck, Ivory Lee, Emily Kunst, Andrew Arduini, and Paul Gellman sat on the living room floor to hand paint and color the *My Molly* covers. "I realized I'd found people who I felt I could dream with… it had been this dream of mine, to be a part of an underground scene like the Dadaists, the Beats, John Cage, and the Happenings. There were always a lot of people around in my childhood. Our house was a stopover for relatives arriving here from Korea.

"And it was like, most of these people around me now also *did art*. I'd moved into the space with the intention of fooling around and sharing ideas and I thought, OK, we're gonna use it to show our art work! I knew that people wanted to meet other people. Just from hanging out with them, I knew this group of musicians had very great artistic

inclinations, not just music but visual art, performance, and writing, and I thought it would be great
to just share that."

Between Tiny Creatures' first show, an untitled
exhibition of collages and drawings by Ariel Pink
and Andrew Arduini that opened on September 16,
2006, and the closing that took place just over two
years later, Kim would produce ten full-scale
gallery shows, dozens of readings, release parties,
art theory symposia, film screenings, performances,
and an 87 page 'zine. The group would travel to the
Pueblo Nuevo community in Mexicali, Mexico to
stage a guest exhibition at Mexicali Rose, an
inspired community gallery founded by Marco
Vera just a few steps from the Mexican side of the
border. Tiny Creatures would be mentioned in
*Artforum*; the *Los Angeles Times* would lament its
closing. Rock stars would stand outside on the
sidewalk as crowds cycled through the small space
which had become a must-see for out of town dealers
and curators

At first glance, the Tiny Creatures' success suggests
a déjà vu on par with the photos. Didn't China Art
Objects, Chinatown's very first gallery founded in
1999 by artists Steve Hanson and Giovanni Intra, go
on to receive miles of slavish admiring coverage from
*Vogue, Elle,* and *W*? Hanson and Intra were as sincere
as Kim in their desire to found a community. But,
burdened by MFA student loan debt, they were also

sincere in their desire for that community to achieve art world fame and viability.

These intentions were never so clear (or clearly shared) by the artists who gathered around Tiny Creatures. As Rachel Detroit remembers, "Tiny Creatures was a continuous thing. It was pretty much the same group, like a little club of cool people but Janet actually put on the shows. People always say they're gonna do shit, but when Janet Kim *says* she's gonna put on a show, even though she's dealing with the most freakish people, the most loose cannons, she always nets them in somehow. She cracks the whip on these freaks!"

Or, as Geneva Jacuzzi recalls, "A lot of these people, our friends, are musicians and they're people who are so creative, they have all kinds of little projects. Maybe they haven't gone through a BA or an MFA degree but they have all this great art—literature, music, visual art. Tiny Creatures was great because it opened itself as a forum to artists who weren't aware of their own ability to be artists. Courtney [Yates, Jacuzzi's sister, one of the Tiny Creatures exhibitors] never went to art school and there's this stigma that if you want to be an artist, you have to get your MFA at an art school. It's very intimidating. Courtney was young at the time but she had all this amazing work, all this talent, and presenting her work was fantastic. To see your work on the wall and realize, That's all it is! It just has to be presented in some form, and then you're pretty much considered an artist. It gives you the ego boost you need if you want to take it further. I liked the fact that it was so easy to get to that point with Tiny Creatures. It was so open. Janet was especially excited about that. She'd come up to me and say, *I want to put your stuff up in the gallery*, and I was like—really? I didn't consider it art—but I guess it is! Some of the work was stuff people had been doing since before high school, and it would go up on the wall even if it wasn't 'good.' That was for everyone else to judge and decide."

At 628 N. Alvarado, friendships would reach an ecstatic pitch and then fall apart. Artists would spend entire months producing 'zines full of interviews and reviews that on the one hand sought to mythologize each other's work, but at the same time questioned the whole idea of art careers built upon "gateway drugs to success" and "authenticity." The group was never wholly on-message. Casual drug use would blossom to crippling habits and some of the artists would be arrested. "It just started out as one thing," Kim recalls, "and then it became something else."

The website would expire. Some of the artists would go on to receive mainstream representation while others would not, although most of the people concerned remain atypically gracious about this phenomenon.

# 2.

*For a long time, they were just working there in the dark, without any thought of outside recognition...*

— Gert Schiff on Zurich Dada and Cabaret Voltaire

The grand opening of Tiny-Creatures-the-Gallery, held at 6 p.m. on September 16, 2006, was less than auspicious. Or then again, maybe more: The evening lasted until 8 the next morning even though nobody came.

The exhibition, named *Untitled* by Kim and *live birth* on a Matt Fishbeck flyer, featured drawings, collage, and ephemera produced and collected by Ariel Pink and Andrew Arduini. Fishbeck was slated to play a Holy Shit set at 8 but he didn't go on until after 2 in the morning, because until then there was no audience.

In 2006, Pink was already well-known as a musician. His song *Getting High In The Morning*, released by the independent label Paw Tracks, was receiving daily radio play on KXLU, a new anthem. Visual art was something he'd done since childhood, but building a gallery career was not his priority. In fact, he forgot to show up at the opening. "I don't know if he remembered we were doing the show or not," Kim recalls. Two weeks before he'd given her a big box containing sketchbooks, drawings, and photos that comprised most of his visual *oeuvre*.

Andrew Arduini, described by his friends as "a genius... a loner... a recluse," was best known for his four-track recordings of musicians he admired, released on CDs as Vibe Central. When Kim first met Arduini, he lived in a motorhome called Georgie Boy, but in the weeks or months preceding the show the van was impounded and, Kim recalls, "By that time he was already homeless. So I went over to the place where he was staying and looked through a box of his stuff and said, *OK, we'll show this, and this.* Later on, he brought more work over."

Photographs of this first installation depict a series of 20-plus drawings by Pink attached to a long wall with pushpins and paperclips. Pink's drawings—made in pencil and ink, featuring intricate calligraphy and grotesque human/animal bodies—are interspersed with found and personal photographs by both of the artists. A hand-adorned *My Molly* EP sits on a shelf beside a sawn-off stuffed squirrel with a long, skinny tail that Kim found and glued onto the wall. The opposite wall features an assortment of Arduini ephemera: a self-published book called *the areas*; a snapshot of the lost motorhome; bubble wrap; an old transistor radio decorated with the Vibe Central logo. There was also an extraordinary sculpture by Arduini: a set of three hand-decorated Vibe Central CD covers arranged in a Cornell-ish wood box, strangely erotic and creepy.

By 8 p.m. Kim, White, Arduini and Fishbeck were still alone in the gallery. Pink hadn't shown and neither had anyone else. "But Ariel eventually came," Kim recalls. "Matt dragged him over… he was living far off, in Beverly Glen, in his Dad's apartment complex and he didn't have a car. But when he saw the show, he was excited."

The five friends hung out for the rest of the night listening to music and talking. At some point their friends Nic Amato and Michael Stock stopped by with gifts but it wasn't until 2 that an actual audience—three people Kim knew from Chicago who'd gone to the Art Institute—arrived and Fishbeck started his set, which Kim remembers as dazzling. One of the girls from Chicago started singing along "and it just kept going." At some point during the night, White snapped a portrait of Arduini, Fishbeck, and Kim bathed in blue light in the main room. Fishbeck wore a cravat, Kim wore a pith helmet, and Arduini leaned on a cane. The three stared at the camera, supremely indifferent about hosting a party in which nobody came.

Around 6, everyone sat on the floor and read Arduini's new literary fiction *God's Masseuse* out loud as the sun rose. When they went home at 8 in the morning, everyone felt like they'd witnessed or given *live birth*, Fishbeck's bootleg title fulfilled.

## 3.



*Why did everybody go down the art street? Suddenly,
it was available... Janet had rent to pay and she
thought: I'm gonna use this space for all it's worth...
Selling art, putting on gigs and charging people for
gigs—it was a very tricky operation.*

— Matt Fishbeck

Almost immediately, Kim started planning the next
Tiny Creatures show. Opening on November 6, it
featured two Fishbeck photo collages, ink drawings
and collages by Ellen Nguyen, and found object ear-
rings by a duo called Rabiez and Rubiez. As artist
Paul Gellman would later observe, "What all these
people do best is collage. They're all on speed, and
people on speed make the best collages since the
'60s!" (This fact would also account for some of the
problems that later emerged.)

Kim met Nguyen through White. Though not a
musician herself, Nguyen regularly attended the
Part Time Punks club nights. She'd recently finished a CalArts film MFA, an experience that left
her virtually paralyzed wherever film was concerned.
Supporting herself as a graphic artist, she'd begun
making personal collages and drawings. Kim liked
Nguyen. She liked the work, and this was a chance
to support it. Given her first opportunity to exhibit
her nonfilmic work, Nguyen installed a series of
small exquisitely framed pieces beside an enormous

self-portrait painted onto the gallery wall: a young Asian woman with a phantom hand reaching into her cupid-shaped mouth. Later, Nguyen would go on to produce sparse, emotionally sumptuous charcoal studies depicting relaxed and distressed fragments of human bodies, presented at Tiny Creatures' 2007 *Summer Retrospective.*

Fishbeck's two stunning digital prints were composed on an old PC program: photos collaged and slightly distorted towards the point of hallucination. As Kim recalls, "Matt showed up with his work an hour before the show and it was hard to install. The prints were 8 feet tall and we didn't know how to install anything. We had no tools." Fishbeck ran out to a car repair yard for some rope—"it looked like licorice." Kim buttressed the prints with bean cans and bricks, "but it worked—they stayed up all night!"

The opening featured performances by Devon Williams and Mountain Girl, a South American woman no one knew well who'd arrived in LA and opened a Chinatown gallery. This time a lot more people showed up. Fishbeck had spent the days preceding the opening passing out handmade flyers in Chinatown.

"Tiny Creatures wouldn't have happened without Matt Fishbeck," the artist Jason Yates observed. "He was the catalyst. I think of him occupying the same space as Malcolm McLaren. Nothing would have happened without his encouragement."

"Something worked," Kim recalls.

Chinatown, Echo Park... in 2006, Chinatown's two dozen-odd galleries planned their openings to occur on the same night. Every three or four weeks the two central Chinatown plazas were thronged by hipsters, collectors, celebrities, artists, and dealers ... everyone who mattered in the Los Angeles art world and many more gathered in crowds that could number a thousand or more. Pioneered by MFA graduates, Chinatown was still the epicenter of Los Angeles art. It was where nearly all the new MFA grads wanted to show, and everyone knew you could not *get* a show unless you were part of that crowd. To this day Gellman questions his decision to move to LA after finishing art school on the East Coast. "I think you should go to school where you want to end up," he reflects. "In terms of connections and shows? In that sense moving out here didn't help me at all."

So it was sort of a triumph when Fishbeck— brilliant, sophisticated and MFA-less; a person who, until then, had never particularly thought of himself as a visual artist—received invitations to mount two solo Chinatown gallery shows. Kim saw Tiny Creatures' potential to serve as a launching pad from her community to the larger world. *TINY CREA- TURES is making this small community of Los Angeles artists available to the wider world, or perhaps, the wider world available to us*, she wrote.

"There was no money anywhere," recalls Fishbeck, who was then living in a garage he shared with another artist. "Suddenly you're a visual artist. It was a way out of poverty. You can sell a CD for $10, but you can sell a picture for as much as you want."

But it wasn't until the third show, Kim tells me, that Tiny Creatures really took off. Curated by No Age, a young band from the underage venue Smell, the show was titled *Get Hurt*. Rachel Detroit, a tall, lean musician in her late 30s, remembers Smell as "an incredible venue. The employees were all volunteers, the kids who hung out there. Punk kids, kids of doctors and lawyers coming in from the Valley, all kinds of kids." The people from No Age made art as well.

*Get Hurt* was an assemblage of watercolors, band flyers, photos, pages ripped out of spiral notebooks and taped to the wall, and an incredible fluorescent painting of people and monsters with dozens of eyes.

"This time," she says, "Tiny Creatures was PACKED. There were so many people. It was already crowded at Ellen and Matt's but at this one, the sidewalk was packed too. There were all of these kids, and also adults with babies and dogs—Devendra [Banhart] *knew* people from New York. They brought people from New York, they knew people somehow."

Kim had already started hosting smaller events to draw people to Tiny Creatures—film screenings, a yard sale, a bratwurst and beer fest, "because other-wise who's gonna come?" The stage was well set for Jason Yates' April, 2007 exhibition entitled *Burnout, The Fast Friends Inc. Project, A Depiction of DIY Dandyism and Pop by Cult Hero Jason Yates.*

Yates is an exceptional artist. For six years as Fast Friends he created band posters for Pink, Fishbeck, and others that are also original art works. Any study of the confluence between music and visual culture in the last two decades would cite Yates' work.

Raised (like Rachel Detroit) in Detroit, he became a friend and collaborator of jazz-fusion musician George Clinton while he was still in his teens. "I've always thought of George Clinton not as a musician but as a total artist," he said on the phone. Yates, in his late 30s, now lives in a beach town near San Diego with his wife and child. "As much as the art world endeavors to branch out, it's still very specialized. To Clinton, making art was part of his normal trajectory. He was an artist-musician. And I always saw art as being a component of a lot of different movements, and incredibly dependent on a group dynamic. The average art writer is lost when it comes to talking about my work with Fast Friends because they don't have that grasp of culture."

Moving to LA in the '90s to study with Mike Kelley, Mayo Thompson, and Liz Larner at Art

Center's MFA program, Yates hung out with musicians but remained very rigid about *not* playing in a band. "It was very important to me that my focus was art," he explains.

Still, though he was hired to teach in an Arizona MFA program after Art Center, his work had yet to be picked up by a gallery. Yates founded Fast Friends to put out his work his own way. Before Tiny Creatures, he had yet to have a solo show in LA.

Looking at images from Yates' *Burnout* exhibition alongside the *Get Hurt* documentation, I'm struck by the intangible quality that differentiates art from ephemera. Both shows featured works composed from the same materials, in similar styles. Both bodies of work orchestrate collisions of signifiers drawn from the same bank of cultural references. Yet Yates' magnificent posters, produced in irregular editions, are decidedly *works of visual art*. In *Shit Age* (2007), witchy pyramid triangles cut out of Mylar surrounded by rivers of watery brush-strokes are infested by animal eyes, pot seeds and pills lie buried in globs of glittery glue… the deranged menagerie seemingly supported on a nest of hatched lines. Weed-green rods of lightening burst out of the sky. "The posters were all infused with inside jokes, inside critiques, inside information," Yates explains. "Because there's a power dynamic between, uh—I really got into using pyramids at that time." The poster Kim shows me is great and I wish it was mine.

"Jason explained," Kim remarks while we examine it, "that the black and white lines signify his heroin phase and the eyes represent tweaking." Clearly Yates was experimenting with just *how far* he could push a stoner aesthetic into the realm of high art. "Ahhh, they were all in the honeymoon phase of their habits," Gellman recalls.

*Burnout* was the first (and last) solo show at Tiny Creatures. The press release helpfully listed Yates' influences (Mike Kelley, Kurt Schwitters, Robert Smithson, Jim Shaw), his artistic lineage (from Dada to Situationism to Fluxus), and art school credentials. Ariel Pink performed at the opening and once again, it was mobbed. This time the work sold—not later in Chinatown, but straight out of the gallery. Which was both good and bad.

One group member recalls, "Janet sold some of Jason's work that really *I* was selling ... I was representing him on the Westside to patrons who had a relationship with me. I was cut out of the deal and then Janet blamed me for bringing this outsider in and allowing Jason to sell pieces off of her wall without her getting anything for it."

"The Jason Yates show was very hot," Gellman remembers. "All kinds of people were there, and for sure he's an interesting artist. But the same old story gets told over and over... everyone's pure, noncommercial, and then they see the chance for a break. But Janet Kim has no connections to money or people who buy things."

As Yates himself sees it, "Collectively we were the hippest thing in the country. Janet Kim… doesn't care about money. We were all broke and people were burning up wanting the work. Janet could have stepped up and made everybody a lot of money. You know? I was having a kid, things were financially desperate and she wouldn't compromise on that, she wouldn't return phone calls. I was like, Janet, we all trust you to take this to the next level and she just folded under the pressure, she didn't have that skill set. And she wouldn't listen to anyone else!"

"Jason Yates is a dick, or, he *can* be a dick," Kim reflects. "I don't know… they were all really critical in ways I just did not understand."

Geneva Jacuzzi and Holy Shit played sets at the closing. Everyone knew this was cooler than Chinatown and people hung out on the sidewalk taking turns going inside.

4.

> *tiny creatures is*
> *a desire to find a way to live our own way*
> *to have a sense of community,*
> *to see each other while on earth,*
> *to share our lives, our pain, our talents, our thoughts,*
> *to capture a moment in time that will be lost or forgotten,*
> *and to package it with beauty, love, pain, and all that*
> *we can feel as humans.*

> — Janet Kim, Tiny Creatures Manifesto 2007

In late May, Tiny Creatures intern Drew Denny organized *Can't Help It*, a collective debut of Los Angeles artists born in the same year, 1984. Prior to graduating from USC's film school, Denny traveled throughout the third world taking photos of labor and agricultural reform movements. Eclectically educated, none of the *Can't Help It* participants had attended MFA programs. As Denny wrote, "Noting the stereotypes of Hollywood, these young artists have conspired to convert the ego into a more encompassing and evasive experience…" This time, the show had a price list.

Busy recording the first Tiny Creatures LP, Kim gave Denny a free hand, but she remembers an art talk in which Eli Langer, a painter, discussed the phenomenology of lines in Otis BFA-grad artist Kate Stewart's work. "I remember being called from the back, *Janet, you've got to come here, it's getting chaotic!* They were doing cocaine and talking about lines—doing lines and talking about lines. I've never heard people talk so much about lines, it was funny and fun."

That summer Kim organized a retrospective featuring work by friends old and new: Ariel Pink, Matt Fishbeck, Ellen Nguyen, Kate Hall, Andrew Arduini, Paul Gellman, and Emily Ryan. By now Tiny Creatures was on the map. Artists and dealers from Chinatown routinely showed up to check the work out. But the confluence of money and drugs was already taking its toll. The Jason Yates show ended with a screaming fight between Yates and Kim about whose Creature it was. "We were getting under each other's skin because everyone was ego fighting, trying to get as much light as they could from the little light that was there, and trying to make money 'cuz everyone was broke," Kim recalls. The feral quality that gave Tiny Creatures its charm would sometimes erupt in fistfights and broken jaws. The core group at this time was using hard drugs and others outside it felt outclassed and snobbed.

It was in this climate that Kim produced her first Manifesto. "Tiny Creatures is not a gallery… is not a venue… a label… Tiny Creatures is a community center… glorifies expression and communication, not the ego… Tiny Creatures is not to be used to commodify art or music, but… as an instrument of communication."

Each artist would be required to sign the manifesto before hanging their work.

"Janet and Ben both had these Christian backgrounds," Paul Gellman recalls. "The organizational style was almost a Christian Youth kind of thing, rallying up the troops."

"I realized," she says, "that people might have different ideas what the space was and I just wanted to clarify what they were getting into."

The retrospective closed with the launch of a 'zine that marked the first year of the space.

5.


*We never pay attention to the mail.*
*Sunshine we hate, it doesn't mean a thing*
*Let others join the struggle to survive*
*Dead to the world, dreaming on our feet*
*The darkness just comes down in sheets.*

— Emmy Hennings, *Morphine*, Zurich 1921

The coming months saw a series of guest-curated exhibitions: *Churchmusic/Lawnpaintings*, *Soft Bodies*, *Tough Creatures*, and *The Three Burritos*. While the explosion of sometimes-conflicting energies around *Burnout* and *Retrospective* led the core group to take a step back, the space was established and younger people arrived, creating a community eclectic beyond Kim's initial dreams. San Diego pro-skaters Spanky and Jerry Hsu exhibited artwork in *The Three Burritos*. The vegan collective Crops and Rawbers turned the space into a temporary restaurant. As Kim recalls, "These shows had a huge impact on Tiny Creatures, because they brought in the young kids, the little Mexican punk kids, the bikers, the skaters, the vegans, and mixed them all in with the older art people. That was the deal."

In May 2008, Kim returned as a curator with *Shitty Hippy: A Collection of Cut-Ups and Freak Outs, Sound, Sculpture, Painting, and Collage Featuring Echo Park-based Artists and Underground Musicians.* Perhaps unwittingly referencing Paul Thek's landmark wax sculpture *Death of a Hippie*, the show was a triumph. Featuring work by Jed Ochmanek, Courtney Yates, Geneva Jacuzzi, Paul Gellman, and others, *Shitty Hippy* was a kind of manifesto for the Tiny Creatures collaged, DIY aesthetic. In an incisive (but still unpublished) catalogue essay, Paul Gellman wrote:

"Good Collage/Assemblage involves inserting one language into another… juxtaposing and playing with contrasting imagery from the culture at large. From Dada through… the punk era, one finds elements of transgression and mystery created through putting disparate images together…

"Being a good collage/assemblage artist requires being a good scavenger. As you walk down the filthy streets outside of your hovel you are probably feeling depressed because for one you live in a hovel, or you are affecting an air of the disaffected, or you are experiencing a fall out from some drug you've been binging on for the past weekend, week, month… Use your downward gaze as an opportunity to see the beautiful detritus that our polluted city offers… Begin to see recurring themes, colors, shapes in the pieces of trash your eye is drawn to. If you are attracted to something, it is because in some way it represents you and the more you learn about yourself the more freedom you have from said hovel…

"Craft counts. And I'm not talking about being archival either, that's for the pussies that think they're leaving their legacy…"

By the end of the summer Kim realized she couldn't maintain Tiny Creatures any more. There was no money. Her credit cards were almost maxed out. Her partner was arrested while buying drugs on Skid Row. Still struggling to meet her friends' expectations that she would promote, sell, and distribute their work, shoplifting, hookers, dealers, and dealing entered the scene.

"It was just very dark. Eventually I never came out of the back. I would just lie in bed smoking and drinking and everyone thought I was this powerhouse alternative curator! I'm not a gallerist… I don't know what they thought. It was supposed to be just a bunch of friends. By then I was old enough to realize if this goes on we're gonna be fucked, we're gonna be homeless. Real estate was just out of control… Drugs added to the excitement of the place. I don't know if I would have done anything different. But it had to stop."

Marco Vera, a friend of Matt Fishbeck and Kim's friend Kelly Coats, had moved back to Mexicali to open a community media center and gallery in late 2006. Kim was in touch with a colleague of Reva's, Gilberto Monreal, about hosting a Softboiled Eggies show at his venue, La Casa de la Tia Tina. When Tia de la Tina—plagued by the same problems that arose at Tiny Creatures—unexpectedly folded, Vera asked Kim if she'd like to arrange a one-night Tiny Creatures event at his space. This, she decided, would be the last show.

Born and raised in the Pueblo Nuevo district of Mexicali, Vera's life opened up when a drunk American driver smashed into his old Chevy Hornet on the Mexican side of the border and ripped off part of his face. He was 16. After paying the plastic surgeon, he used the rest of the settlement money to enroll in film school at San Diego State University. From there, he moved up to LA and found work as a production assistant. To the horror of Vera's family (his father had lived in the then-slummy neighborhood three decades before), he lived in Echo Park where he met other filmmakers at the Echo Park Film Center and became friends with Fishbeck and others at the Little Joy bar.

Vera disliked his work as a film industry production assistant. By 2006 his life in the city had started to pall. "The US felt like a really strange place—the whole building of a new border wall, bad vibes all around; I just felt weird. Even a lot of the friends I had met, it wasn't the same. Echo Park was already starting to be really gentrified, the families I knew who made the neighborhood into a community like Pueblo Nuevo were getting the boot. So I saved up as much as I could." Vera remembers seeing people outside Janet Kim's storefront as he was leaving LA in a U-Haul, and thinking: *Maybe I shouldn't be leaving. I hope this space is sincere.*

But he'd already conceived of a plan to take over his uncle's old Pueblo Nuevo house and turn it into an audio-visual production workshop for neighborhood kids. The youth of Pueblo Nuevo include both children of residents and effectively transient young people who arrive from the south and move between border towns.

Vera, then 28, spent three months evicting the low-level smugglers who'd moved into the house and more than six months fixing it up. As soon as it opened, the space took off. The workshops expanded to include neighborhood parents. Artists wanted to exhibit their work at the space, so Vera turned several rooms into a gallery. Since then Mexicali Rose has become a hybrid border community all its own. The kids in Vera's workshop have produced an astonishing body of experimental and documentary video works. Edgar Moreno, a pizza delivery boy, strapped a video camera onto his bike to create a poetic montage of city lights that struck me as more accomplished than most MFA-program neo-structuralist films. Vera's recent exhibition, *Puro Personaje*, featured found and original photos by local kids, art students at Mexicali's UABC, professional artists and architects, and lost souls from US border towns like Brawley and El Centro who gravitate to the space.

The Los Angeles artist George Porcari and I drove down for the show and found the opening more like a block party. In LA openings tend to be targeted networking stops on a five-or-six gallery crawl, but this was Mexicali's Friday night out, with sangria punch and plates of food and Peruvian psychedelic music from the '60s and '70s blasting on the PA. Neighborhood girls in tight jeans and their boyfriends got out of cars. A guy from the state museum explained some of the town's cultural politics. It went on 'til 2.

Thirteen Los Angeles artists contributed work to the Mexicali show, which Fishbeck titled *Under Alvarado: There Is A Beach*, a pun on the name of the Spanish explorer who served as Cortez's right hand in the conquest of Mexico and Mexicali's scorching Sonora desert. Most of the artists traveled down for the opening on November 15, 2008, and Fishbeck, joined by local musicians, played a Holy Shit set. "Everyone was really high in Mexicali," he recalls. One of the Echo Park artists had just been let out of jail for assault, but the show was an ecstatic success. The opening ended with Paul Gellman playing heavy metal on Fishbeck's guitar. Two years later, I sit in Vera's cool dark editing room and watch the 8-minute film of that night.

When Kim returned to LA more chaos ensued: more drugs, more debt, more arrests. *REALITY IS MONEY*, she wrote in her diary… *we can rob a bank.* She gave notice to move out but realized she couldn't leave 628 N. Alvarado without staging one last show. *YOU ARE INVITED TO BE THE LAST tiny creature*, the invite said. This time, 26 artists contributed work. The *Los Angeles Times'* photo feature on the January 10, 2009, closing party looks like a portrait of the new LA: neurosurgeons, fashion designers, visitors from London, curators, musicians, and local artists stand outside with drinks, just a few yards away from a spot near the freeway where homeless men still sell oranges.

"Tiny Creatures did what it set out to do. … It refuses to be big. If it were bigger, it would no longer be Tiny Creatures. … Tiny Creatures is an alternative to an overly commodified world… There can be change, change in Tiny Creatures ways, change in tiny ways," Kim wrote in her final manifesto.

That night Paul Gellman covered one wall of the kitchen with blank paper and everyone pitched in to create one last collaborative artwork.

As Hedi El Kholti, one of the contributing artists, recalls, "The show was an event, for sure. There were a lot of people and it seemed much more 'ambitious' than previous manifestations. The work was well installed and the show was coherent. 'More established artists' like Eli Langer, Skylar Haskard, and Michael Rashkow contributed work that had some of the same collage, found-object quality Paul Gellman talks about. It was the end, but it could just as well have been the beginning of something else, on the verge of being professionalized or branded like, say, Aaron Rose's Beautiful Losers. You know the book *Auto-Dissolution of the Avant-Gardes* by René Lourau?

Instead of publishing the manifestos written when they start, he compiled the manifestos of why they need to end their projects. I don't know. I remember feeling sad about it that night—like, that's the last time I'll be young, and I mean by that a more ambiguous relationship with time and productivity."

"I guess if you look at it from outside, if you want, you can see a beginning, middle, and end," Geneva Jacuzzi told me this summer. "But that's not how it was. If you're in the middle of it, you just see time passing and events. It did change. But it would go off and on, depending on what artists were there. Janet Kim is a real artist. It was fun, it was a good time. It was hip for a minute in Echo Park."

"To me, what was important was these kids had not gone to grad schools and stuff," Paul Gellman says. "They were musicians who made art on the side, unappreciated art…"

I suggest to Kim that Vera's project, undertaken in a Mexican *barrio* neighborhood with people already connected in many ways, might be better suited to creating a more lasting community—but she doesn't agree.

For that matter, neither does he, "I don't know if Mexicali Rose is setting out to make a more lasting community either," Vera emailed me later. "The dynamic and situations Tiny Creatures developed are quite different from ours, despite having so much in common. The sentiment of that place and time was so mutual between most of the people involved that it was unspoken as all those moments were being lived out in Echo Park."

Still, Kim doesn't think she'll undertake anything like Tiny Creatures in the near future. She's writing new songs (one of them for Ariel Pink's Haunted Graffiti) and teaching early music notation. She opens a book and shows me the thick square notes on ancient scales from the 14th century written down by the monks.

Four weeks later when I send her a draft of this story, she tells me she's just accepted an invitation to curate a new Tiny Creatures show later this year.

2

THE COMPLETE POEM /

BERNADETTE CORPORATION

Invited to produce an exhibit in September 2009 at Greene Naftali, a commercial gallery in Chelsea, the Bernadette Corporation (a floating "collective" whose principal members in this case were Bernadette Van-Huy, Jim Fletcher, John Kelsey, and Antek Walczak) quickly decided the show would consist of two elements: a series of mostly black and white fashion photographs hung on the walls promoting an unidentified product, and a long epic poem of some 130-plus pages entitled *A Billion and Change*. All of Bernadette Corporation's projects are epic. I asked the poet Eileen Myles how she defines an epic poem and she said, "The world is an epic poem."

Since beginning their work together in 1994, Bernadette Corporation has produced several issues of *Made in USA*, a fashion and cultural magazine; *Get Rid of Yourself*, a feature-length documentary centered around the Genoa antiglobalization riots;

*Reena Spaulings*, a collectively written novel about a 20-something protagonist whose modeling debut in an underwear shoot is disrupted by a natural disaster; as well as occasional writings and videos. Adopting their name as "the perfect alibi for not having to fix an identity" at a moment when branding was the buzzword in fashion, Bernadette Corporation has always looked to the fashion world as a template or mirror of the cultural industry at large. As Antek Walczak remarked after the show at Green Naftali, "What are people's problems with fashion? There's a blind spot—people think fashion is uniquely superficial, as if everything else is not."

Marked by their off-kilter blankness, the fashion spreads published in *Made in USA* featured zombied models in mirrored glasses posed in disarrayed rooms. Bernadette Corporation has always maintained a complex relation to blankness. In its 2001 videotape *Hell Frozen Over*, critic and theorist Sylvère Lotringer stands on a frozen mid-winter lake describing the *white space* of Mallarme's poems while the image-track cuts to a fashion shoot in a loft and this is never ironic because all forms of blankness contain some kind of beauty. As Bennett Simpson astutely noted in "Techniques of Today," his essay on Bernadette Corporation's earlier work, "In a cultural landscape littered with 'alternatives'… Bernadette Corporation were quick to see identity as a fallacious term usurped by capital—and so they sought to undermine it from within."

The 38 fashion photographs created for Bernadette Corporation's show at Greene Naftali featuring three boys and three girls in generic denim styles are hilarious, glamorous, troubling. Shot against a blank background, the models are grouped in a series of casual psychodynamic tableaux. Styled and shot for Bernadette Corporation by fashion photographer David Vasiljevic, they reprise a real-life Levi's campaign Vasiljevic produced for an ad agency. But in this incarnation, the images live by themselves. No captions or ad copy are superimposed and the clothing worn by the models is brandless.

"We were brainstorming for a kind of imagery, a strange material, to introduce an epic poem," Bernadette Van-Huy remarked. "When we saw the campaign David shot for Levi's a year ago, we knew it was what we wanted. First, the generic and expansive aura and subtext of the jeans campaign, and in particular, David's brand of imagery." Cut adrift from their commercial function, the images matter-of-factly expose fashion photography's potent but limited bag of tricks for conflating youth and "lifestyle."

Six individuals present themselves in a series of poses and what do we see? Sex, class, and race; race, class, and sex in a fresh configuration. Gone are the CK and Benetton multihued models of uniform classical beauty from ad campaigns of the '90s. Three of Vasiljevic's primary models are strictly white trash—a *Jules and Jim* trio consisting of a studly, bare-chested blonde in torn jeans, his nondescript brunette pal, and a slutty white girl whose plump lips always default to a pout. The fourth model—a tough-femme Filipina—remains alert, dressed, and always within her own world. Art direction succeeds to the extent that it locks down our fleeting perceptions of an ambient present into coherent images. There's an amazing potential contained in that freeze.

In 2009, color is smart, color is power, color is cool. Kneeling in a thicket of four male denimed legs (the better to give a blowjob or two) and staring wide-eyed into the lens, the white girl's clothes are arranged to display soft bulges of fat. With the blonde's bulging crotch to her right and a skateboard to the left of her face, her sports bra is gently pulled up to reveal an inch of her tits as her ass rides out of her jeans. Vasiljevic's Caucasians project a sullen stupidity graced by an impossible beauty that's destined to fade before they're out of their teens. Like all models in ad campaigns, the product is really themselves—and by extension, a life in jeans.

*Youth is very strapping.*
*These bodies are flexible and full of cum.*
*But it's sad to work like a whore.*
*Let's have some fighting spirit.*
*— A Billion and Change*

Critique and desire. Like all of Bernadette Corporation's work, the pictures are somewhat ironic but more importantly they are always simultaneously true. Their epic poem speaks to that fact, among hundreds of others:

*Nothing is one thing, only simultaneously*
*A motorcycle is buzzing and my mom is somewhere.*
*It's six o'clock in the morning, and it's three o'clock in the*
*morning.*
*What are you doing simultaneously?*

The job of the poem, it could be said, is to describe the present. And poetry has always been the dark, secret heart of Bernadette Corporation's work. Pre-Bernadette Corporation, working odd jobs after college, Fletcher and Kelsey rented an office in the then-warehouse district of Chelsea and set themselves up as "The Agency." Their principal job was writing (mostly unpublished) collaborative poetry. When the Bernadette Corporation formed several years later, this métier of group work was already familiar. "Mock incorporation is quick and easy," they wrote at the time. "No registration or fees, simply choose a name (i.e., Booty Corporation, Bourgeois Corporation, Buns Corporation) and spend a lot of time together. Ideas will come later."

Relentlessly intervening at cultural moments over a decade, all of Bernadette Corporation's subsequent work can best be described as a kind of gestural poetry. Their various projects have mobilized strands of ideas and experience into provocative gestures that—like the best poems—avoid programmatic critiques and their implicit, misleading "solutions." This is why Bernadette Corporation is so cool. Their thinking is deeply political, but unlike "political" art, Bernadette Corporation's projects seek to capture the present and amplify it. Their work—whether in video, visual images, print media, or film—is always (like the best poems) inherently formal. As Kelsey has said, "Form is a weapon. It's something that cannot be argued with."

Bernadette Corporation's decision to produce a long epic poem for the Greene Naftali exhibit was a radical move towards transparent clarity, though it was sadly misunderstood by much of its audience in the art world. They've always been poets! Why not produce an actual poem? The job of great poetry has always been stating the obvious in all its complexity. This can be terrifying. And, as Bernadette Corporation found, it was especially terrifying to visual artists, whose miscomprehension of poetry rivals the philistine mantra of mid-century dentists—"My four-year-old could have done that!"—when looking at paintings by Abstract Expressionists.

"Is it a… *real* poem," art colleagues asked at the opening. "Is it sincere, or is it a parody? Is it—umm, any *good*?"

*A Billion and Change* is a great poem, astonishing in its formal range and ambition. Aided by a series of Oulipian constraints, the poem is lyrical, imagist, fabulist, willfully dumb, reportorial, profound, but most of all accurate in its insistence upon understanding a world situation—the "economic collapse"—through four or five bodies:

*1 tuna salad sandwich on white, 1 roast beef sandwich on Italian, 1 small bottle of water, $16.50. Dr. Bidi says blue is the color of war. Today the trees and posts turn blue in the sun… A creek the color of coke…*
    *Hate is often fused with a fear. Someone doesn't hate*
*A person just because a person sucks more or less.*
*Wishing pain or their death is such a rarer feeling.*
*Brute hate.*
*The present turns into a sort of long daily walk.…*

For dozens of pages, the poem turns on the formal conceit of "branding" the text by including words beginning with the letters *B* and *C* in each skinny line—

    *What's the beautiful chorus*
*I hear while basting my capers*
*It's Bellini on the CD. …*

—but its real triumph is its insistent return to the dailiness that has always been the raw material of poetry.

Unlike Bernadette Corporation's collaborative novel *Reena Spaulings*, an assemblage written by dozens of people all over the world during more than a year, *A Billion and Change* grew from the compressed effort of four or five people meeting to write together a few times a week over the summer. By sheer proximity (and a lot of shared history) the poem, though written in turns by individuals, assumes a single collective voice.

*Our little we against the American I sometimes*
*The city is a rat's vagina in a good way.*

As Jim Fletcher recalls, "A lot of the writing happened in the meetings. Ideas started to take shape, but still we had nothing. We were inspired by Mallarmé, his writing on fashion... not because of fashion per se, but because of the writing. And writing is an object. The idea was, we wanted to make it an epic poem. Not a 'collection.' But what was an epic poem? And what do we want? It wasn't like, 'what idea do we have?' It was more, 'what does the poem want?' There's this strong feeling we've had about poetry—it's the juice, we love it—but what is it about poetry that bugs me? You want to do battle, you want to wage war on it—but then you look at a lot of poems that are published, and it could be a really excellent poem with burning great sentences, but what you really see is, where was it published? And then somebody's name at the bottom."

*Porn is very popular*
*On line we saw tits, amateurs, young sex and anal sex*
*In a bar, everyone has seen porn, it's really obvious*
*Let's decide everything is porn…*

"We started looking at epic poems. Gertrude Stein's *Stanzas in Meditation*—it's a very long poem, and it has its own way of ordering language, but anything can go in it. It has that kind of scope. It doesn't have to take place in a single day or recount a single event, but in a way, there *is* an event, and that's the event of the poem and that time. We thought about that a lot. What does an epic have? What defines it? It's TIME. That was what we had to work with."

*Pay Seth.*
*Send Hedi cover image.*
*R: Re: Rif: question.*
*Get specs/sketches to the marble people.*
*Ask Helene to measure the heaters in Brussels.*
*Blighted oaks present untold hazards…*

"A time and a place, New York," Fletcher continues. "It's so hard to place, but epic means letting it in. The epic is open, it's perforated. And there's a huge advantage to writing with several people… the perforation is built right in, and also their histories together, and relationships. Our relationships with each other are very much part of the explosive force of the thing. Everybody in the group means so much to me, it's almost like an ongoing crisis. We decided to focus our writing skills on this thing. It was extremely exciting, the way it gets out of your hands. You can't really say That Section Came From That Person—it came so much out of discussion, and everyone had a side pass at every single part of it, and a lot of it was written in group ways right there in the room."

Displayed in a series of 13 custom-built vitrines, Bernadette Corporation's epic poem filled the gallery. At first viewing, I spent nearly two hours bent at the waist, peering down at its uniform pages to read. The poem—because of its splendor, I kept seeing the world compressed into spare lines—took a long time to read, and this was exciting. I had to keep standing back to let the images settle. In her *New York Times* review of the show, critic Roberta Smith noted the *discomfort* she felt viewing or reading it. Although in her opinion *A Billion and Change* was no "literary landmark," she deemed it a bona fide poem: it was "real," it was "genuine."

But as it turned out, the insertion of poetry, displayed like a work of visual art in a gallery space, was deeply disturbing to most. For years writers have played a circumscribed role in the visual art world. Our job is to write about art; to give it a language that translates into value. Perhaps the only paid, nonteaching job now for poets and nonmainstream American writers is churning out art reviews and catalogue essays for high-profile museum and gallery shows. In the 21st century, art writing plays the same role as magazine fiction did for mid-20th century writers like Philip K. Dick and Chester Himes. It offers a badly paid livelihood. As Eileen Myles said, "The old exchange has always been poets writing about artists. And that was always contingent on the poet being interested in the artist's production, and the marketplace bringing them together."

Audaciously, Bernadette Corporation insisted on treating the 130-plus pages of *A Billion and Change* as an original artwork. No press copies, no posting online, no Xeroxed handouts. As John Kelsey recalls, "Some of our most politically correct friends were outraged that we weren't passing the poem out for free or putting it online. And artist friends basically say, 'art should be for sale, writing should be for free.' It's crazy how this conventional distribution of labor and value persists, even among smart people. As a sometime art writer who gets paid shit for labor, this may be a sore point for me, that text backs up and explains the art, but should not share the value of art. Not that the poem was all about this… but it was a real point of contention that arose during our show… poetry should be free."



"One thing we knew," Antek Walczak recalls, "was we didn't want to present the poem as a gallery reading, where everyone comes in and leaves. We didn't want that effortless transmission. The way we ended up doing it, a lot of people weren't sure if it was an art object, and that was good. It's like—here's my poem. We were complaining. It was hard. Sometimes a black cloud came over our heads. It's a sincere poem, same thing as being a serious artist."

"This is the most radical gallery show I've seen in years," I wrote in my notebook after riding the elevator back down to West 26th Street. The conjunction of Vasiljevic's stranded black and white photographs and the vitrine-captured poem turned the gallery space into a vessel of contradiction and mystery. Like everything true, *A Billion and Change* is both sincere *and* a parody. It is "amusing"—that great poet word used to tremendous effect by the late poet Ted Berrigan—and always accurate.

3

NO MORE UTOPIAS

In 2006 Elke Krystufek traveled to Easter Island with her collaborator Donat Orovac. At that time she was investigating the work and the life—or more precisely, the mythology surrounding the work and the life—of the late Bas Jan Ader. Yet in the 33 years of his short life, Jan Ader never set foot on Easter Island.

Born in the Netherlands in 1942, Jan Ader moved to Los Angeles when he was age 19 to attend art school. Exhibiting widely, he mostly remained in LA until his famous departure on a solo journey across the Atlantic in a 13-foot sailboat, which would prove fatal. The voyage was planned as the final installment of his conceptual triptych *In Search of the Miraculous*. He'd been gearing up for this. Part 2 was a choral performance of sea chanteys.

Jan Ader sailed from Cape Cod in July 1975 and was expected in Falmouth about 60 days later, but he never arrived. The artist who'd roamed LA at night with a flashlight in the first work of this series—his search for the miraculous ironically captioned with lyrics from an old Coasters' rock and roll song from the '50s—had vanished. Three weeks into the trip, Jan Ader lost radio contact. As his brother Erick later reported, "On about April 10, 1976, a Spanish fishing trawler found his boat about 150 nautical miles west-south-west of Ireland. It was two-thirds capsized, with the bows pointing down. Judging by the degree of fouling, it looked as though the boat had been drifting around in this position for about six months."

His body was never recovered. The approximate time of his death was divined by measuring avian excrement. A conceptual joke not intended… although as biographer Charles Nicholl noted in *Somebody Else: Arthur Rimbaud in Africa 1880–91*; *Every contact leaves traces.*

Death and disappearance. According to Elke Krystufek, Four words beginning with *F* encapsulate the recurring themes of Jan Ader's work:

Failure
Fragility
Falling, &
Fatalism.


In one of his earliest pieces, Jan Ader produced a postcard that featured a close-up of his tear-stained face. Titled *I'm Too Sad To Tell You*, the image enacted that marvelous, irreducible mixture of genuine sentiment and wry irony. These tears have migrated into Krystufek's work since 2006 when she began her investigation of Jan Ader's legend. They remained on the walls of her *Culture Against Culture* installation at the 2009 Venice Biennial. But by then, the Jan Ader-inspired voyage to Easter Island had led her to investigate an earlier art-disappearance: the improbable South Seas wartime sojourn of the German expressionist Max Hermann Pechstein.

In 1970, the same year he produced *I'm Too Sad To Tell You*, Jan Ader created the whimsically violent *Light* installation/performance. In it, eight cement blocks hovered on ropes above eight impossibly delicate objects: a glass vase of flowers, some pillows, a birthday cake, light bulbs and eggs… and here they remained, until Jan Ader himself cut the ropes, destroying these fragile objects in front of gallery viewers. In his notebook of drawings and diary entries he wrote: *Greetings From Beautiful Ader Falls*. And then he adds, *All is falling*. Later he would continue:

*My body practicing having been drowned.*
*My body practicing being dead.*

Weeks after Jan Ader's demise was presumed, some of his colleagues on the UC Irvine art faculty would open his locker and find a disturbing object or, you could almost say, *message*: a hardback copy of *The*

*Strange Last Voyage of Donald Crowhurst*, a nonfiction account of Crowhurst's attempt to fake a solo non-stop global voyage that began as a prank and ended in madness and drowning.

The seductive romance of the Jan Ader myth was largely forgotten after his death, but revived in the early '90s by conceptual artists who passed it on to their students. Charles Ray sailed a boat in Jan Ader's memory. Christopher Williams memorialized him in *Bouquet for Bas Jan Ader and Christopher D'Arcangelo* (1991). Discussing Jan Ader's persistent appeal with Bruce Hainley in his excellent *Artforum* essay on the artist's influence, Jennifer Bornstein observed: "[Jan Ader's] subject matter is so banal, but the fact that he does it anyway and how it is transformed in execution continues to amaze. Is it manipulated or is it real? He walks such a fine line."

In *Dr. Love on Easter Island* (2006), Krystufek reinvents herself as the character "She-Bas" and wanders the island conducting an off-camera debate with someone called "Dr. Love." Taunting the artist with questions of fame, myth, career and archival value, Dr. Love represents the voice of The Institution. Unlike Jan Ader, She-Bas refuses to die. Withstanding Love's inquisition, she swims in the waves, encounters wild horses, and performs a strange sunset greeting ritual with a local woman. As Krystufek will ask in one of the inspired, wild texts that since 2006 have accompanied her exhibitions, "*Who wants to sail with Bas Jan Ader anyway?*" (*Nein*, 2009).

On the walls of the Austrian Pavilion in Venice—alongside *Culture Against Culture* (2009), a large double portrait of an anonymous nude male model sitting beside the actor Roland Koch—Krystufek wrote:

> *This is the one who may speak to us today*
> *2-morrow it's another one.*
> *This is needed—*
> *This song this Love this documentation*
> **& that one isn't.**

Myth never comes free of its documentation. Myth is an honor that Krystufek has declined, though she's dabbled in it throughout her career by various means, including extravagant self-portraiture. "Don't aggrandize yourself," she warns in the *Nein* manifesto, "except for the common good."

(Hearing the opening bars of the Talking Heads' *Psycho-Killer* dumped onto the soundtrack of Nora Ephron's *Julie and Julia* last month at the multiplex, I was seized by an almost unbearable sadness. You can hear in David Byrne's 19-year-old voice how badly he wanted it. *The future we dream of is always more glorious than the one that transpires.*)

The point, I believe, of Krystufek's continuing project is not that she's made her life into an artwork.

Many lives, many artworks. Rather, it's the *kind* of life she continues to manifest. For nearly two decades, each of the artist's extravagant projects has spontaneously opened new tropes and questions that she invariably picks up and explores in subsequent projects. Her commitment to forging continuity between disparate, disjointed systems is what seems important. In this sense, she's a philosopher, pushing the situations that she creates towards a zany syncretism. While Jan Ader's appeal to the present seems wistfully fey, Krystufek's work is more confrontational: she creates fabulous messes and imparts them with logic through her slapstick presence.

Since her "shocking" 1990 debut when she masturbated to an iconic male rock singer's tape in *Aktion*, her MFA show at Vienna's Fine Art Academy, Krystufek's work has been marked by her hyperappearance. In the beginning, this hyperappearance was explicit and physical, featuring hundreds (or possibly thousands) of gorgeous self-portraits that depicted her every mood and persona. In *The Blue Moods of Spain* (2000), she matter-of-factly undressed before perplexed and uncomfortable spectators at Frankfurt's Portikus Gallery and proceeded to excrete into a large goblet behind a blanket. As she would later note wryly in *Nein,* "It's still interesting to undress for people who absolutely don't want you to."

In 2006, Krystufek abruptly stopped making works that used her presence and image as subjects. Instead, she began painting portraits. But this fascination with portraiture hardly signaled Krystufek's disappearance. Rather, it provided a means for her to expand her palette of multiple selves through the faces of others. Her portraits of Sir John Suckling, Lenny Bruce, Katherine Mansfield, Jack Smith, Tracy Emin, and many others function equally well as *self*-portraits. We are our influences. Similarly, since abandoning solo performance Krystufek has appeared as an actress in the increasingly elaborate video-films that she's produced since 2005, channeling herself through an array of characters.

The romance of disappearance was arguably one of the great organizing myths of the mid-20th century. *To become someone else.* In 1965, Bob Dylan sang, "You lose yourself / You reappear / You suddenly find / You have nothing to fear." In *The Talented Mr. Ripley*, Patricia Highsmith's Tom Ripley kills Dickie Greenleaf in order to assume the more privileged young man's identity. In AMC's *Mad Men*, the poor, white, rural orphan Dick Whitman grabs his dead lieutenant's nametag in the chaotic aftermath of Korean War combat. Reborn as Lt. Don Draper, he finds himself poised to become a player in the postwar consumerist boom, free of his own sad history.

Does disappearance exist? Is it even possible? Describing a photograph of Arthur Rimbaud taken during the third year of his famed "disappearance" into colonial Africa as a trader, Charles Nicholl observes the prescience conveyed in Rimbaud's youthful works:

"Of the man himself, out of the blankness, a few details emerge in poignant clarity: the big sun-darkened hands; the rucks and folds on his trousers; the right leg bent … And in the face itself, though blurred, is a haggardness, a hollowed-out look, a leatheriness—*'lost climates will tan me'*—and a deep but defiant loneliness.

"Comparing these photos with those of the handsome young 'hooligan poet' of Paris, one gets a measure of just how far Rimbaud has come on this journey to become 'somebody else.'"

*THE PAINT*
*BECOMES ALL*
*ENCOMPASSING*
*DIRT creating*
*(teardrop) memories—the*
*painting starts*
*to speak 2 someone*
*        else*

—Krystufek wrote on the wall of the Austrian Venice Pavilion.

Rimbaud's *literary* suicide was by no means an actual suicide. No longer a poet, Rimbaud became completely engrossed in his life as an African trader, explorer and Arabist. Moving farther and farther away from Aden, Somalia's French trading port, and into the African continent, Rimbaud fulfilled the prophecy that he grandiosely pronounced in his *Lettre du Voyant*, written 13 years prior in Paris : *I is somebody else.*

In August 2009 Krystufek traveled to Palau: a group of 210 islands some 500 miles east of the Philippines, encompassing less than 200 square miles. Of these islands, only 10 are inhabited. At the time of its last census in 2005, Palau—a sovereign state that was briefly a German colony at the turn of the 20th century—had a population of 21,000. In 2006 she'd traveled to Easter Island to "confront" the myth of Jan Ader. This time she was retracing the steps of Max Hermann Pechstein, a German Expressionist and decorative artist whose strange trajectory led to these islands.

But whereas Jan Ader had never once visited Easter Island, Pechstein arrived on the Palauan islands in 1914. Devastated by his expulsion from Berlin's Brucke (Bridge) group of Expressionist artists, Pechstein's refugee status was purely psychic.

Influenced equally by their own urban lives and industrial Europe's romance with the primitive, the Brucke group saw their work bridging the rootedness of Europe's agrarian past and the disjunction of the early 20th century. Excluded from showing their work at Berlin's 1911 Secession Exhibit, the group rented a space and staged an alternative show. When Pechstein accepted an invitation to show his own work two years later in the 1913 Secession Exhibit, he was excommunicated.

Taking the Brucke group's primitivist romance very literally, Pechstein chose the Palau islands as his place of exile. But he'd barely arrived when the then-German colony was attacked by Japan in a remote World War I battle. He was captured and interned on Palau by Japanese fighters. Released the following year, Pechstein worked his way to Berlin stoking coal on an ocean steamer, only to be drafted into the German army shortly after arriving.

Most of the work Pechstein produced on Palau was lost in the chaos of wartime. But these unfortunate events of his youth—or the idea of Palau itself—formed an indelible influence. Palau became Pechstein's secret utopia: a prelapsarian state he would strive to recapture for the rest of his life in hundreds of lithographs, drawings, and paintings.

Stricken by a congenital lung ailment ten years later, he produced one of his most famous works, *Femmes des Iles*, a sensuous portrait of a group of Palauian women, which he bartered for treatment at the Montreux Sanitarium.

*HERMANN*
*WHERE*

*R*
*U*
*?*

Krystufek scrawled on the wall of the Venice Pavilion beside *Hescape* (2009), her diptych portrait of a young, non-native male nude posed in front of a teeming blue backdrop of Palauan ocean.

According to Wikipedia.de, "In 1914 Hermann Pechstein traveled to Palau in the South Pacific. He experienced life in a world which he romantically idealized as an earthly paradise without the constraints of European conventions."

The romance of the primitive... but which primitive? Most European expressionist art yearned towards the sharp angular lines of Central African textiles and totems—the rigor and violence evoked in these "primitive" works seen, perhaps, as a cipher for urban Europe's industrial capitalism. But Pechstein's Pacific offers escape. The works are all softness.

In his *Junges Paar im Boot* (1920), a lithograph owned by Germany's Kestner Museum, a man, woman, and baby stand on a boat beneath radiant coconut palms, backlit by a sun so large it's practically smiling. Their limbs are athletic and supple. Other lithographs in this series depict groups of young women (sitting) and young men (fishing). Tucked away behind statuesque palms and verdant tropical foliage, the village meetinghouse in *Dorf in der Sudsee* (1919) evokes a collectivist dream achieved without revolution.

Krystufek's interest in Pechstein's Palauan foray evokes the failed utopias of male expressionists visiting the South Seas... but how did they ever conceive of these tribal locales as utopias? The narrative arc of Murnau's famous 1931 film *Tabu* traces the fall of two young people, Reri and Matahi, from the sacred, implacable cruelty of their indigenous tribe to the cruelty of industrial capitalism. When Matahi sees his beloved Reri about to be sacrificed as a Maid to the Gods, he abducts her and the two flee their remote island for civilization, only to find they need *money*. Reprising Bataille's notion of the Sacred Sacrifice in a popular format, *Tabu* reveals the anonymous cruelty of western capital as more lethal than any primitive rite.

As I write this at the end of 2009, hundreds of links pop up when I type *Palau* into Google. The small nation has just granted asylum to six of the Chinese Muslim Uighurs who have been held by the US at Guantanamo Bay for seven years without legal charges. During the summer a circuit court judge granted the Uighurs legal asylum in the US, but this ruling was challenged and reversed by the Supreme Court. Now, no one knows what to do with the Uighurs. Four have been sent to Bermuda, five to Albania, seven remain at Guantanamo Bay.

Palau received its six Uighurs last weekend, but today the island government issued a statement expressing the hope that Australia will take the six refugees "on a more permanent basis."

Reading further on Google, I find an ad for an unpaid caretaker job at an eco-lodge built (and abandoned) on Palau by two Americans:

*"Though stunningly beautiful we cannot emphasize enough that this is a REMOTE Pacific island. We define remoteness as distance from definitive medical care. There is a nurse on the island. We don't know how thoroughly trained he is but we do know the office is not well equipped... For good medical care you will need to go either to Guam or better yet, Honolulu. The best solution, therefore, is not to get sick or get hurt... There may be cell phone access within the next few months but receiving incoming calls will be nearly impossible. For internet, you will have to go to the school to use a VERY SLOW dial up connection (it's shared by 16 other schools throughout Palau)."*

No island, however remote, exists off the grid of ecological tourism. Therefore, it's wholly appropriate that Krystufek's Palauan nudes depict not Pechstein's idealized natives, but a young, healthy, attractive Euro-male hippie. On the left side of the *Hescape* diptych, his left hand rests in his right open palm in a yogic mudra. The painting is mildly erotic: on the right side—a closer, full-frontal portrait—his penis is fully exposed. But this part of the painting is no less erotic than his steeped-in-thought, downward gaze.

Krystufek produced a short video during her stay in Palau. Just as the earlier *Dr. Love* video tracked her ramblings as She-Bas around Easter Island, the camera now follows a lone male protagonist who may or may not be Hermann Pechstein. During this trip, Krystufek also produced six ink drawings, *Stonehead 1–6*, that depict some of Palau's mysterious rock carvings. Made from the same volcanic stone as the famous Rapanui *moai* sculptures of Easter Island, the provenance of these stoneheads remains unknown to Palau's inhabitants. Though Pechstein's Palauan work mostly portrayed human figures, Krystufek borrows and loosens the artist's decorative style to depict these rock carvings. Krystufek's stoneheads are set deep within tall tufts of tall grass—these stones-in-the-grass are an odd eroticized mirror to the hippie male body in *Hescape*—and the emotional tone of the drawings ranges between benign to ominous. In *Stonehead 1*, one of Pechstein's stray island birds perches atop a rock crevice. Dense *Stonehead 3*, resting under a darkening sky, is more troubled.

Executed with mindful abandon, Krystufek's *Stonehead* drawings revisit Pechstein's expressionist impulse free of the weight that inspired his flight from early 20th century Europe. In Palau, the rocks are still there. *No more utopias.* Of all the contemporary art projects I know of, Krystufek's is the most hopeful.

# 2. Body Not Apart

# MAY '69

Perhaps the greatest promise conveyed by the events of May '68 was the eruption of spontaneity in public life and with it, the idea that—even at this late stage in the consumerist game—it might be possible to live differently. Demonstrations and riots interrupted the dreary process of national politics. For a brief moment, events and ideas—subject to instant revision—occurred in the ecstatic cocoon of a revolution. As Franco Berardi astutely observed in *The Soul at Work*, "the 1968 movements were the first phenomenon of conscious globalization." Structural change of course proved impossible. What remained was a widespread desire to reclaim the personal freedom inhaled—first-hand or vicariously—during those days, *over time*, outside the tempestuous bubble of revolutionary action/reaction. New models for living were needed, new definitions of "normal." For when the barricades were dismantled, the fabric of daily life remained largely unchanged. As Dutch Fluxus artist Willem de Ridder described his postwar generation in 2005, "Our upbringing was death. Father was the boss. Strict rules. The word 'sex' alone was enough to give you a red face." Homosexuality remained illegal throughout the world. Until 1965, married women in the UK were prohibited from having their own bank accounts.

So it isn't surprising that in the ensuing years, the word "liberation" would migrate from a term to describe postcolonial struggles to include all aspects of daily life. Women's liberation, gay liberation, children's liberation… the concept of "liberation" was as central to the ethos of those years as "recovery" is to our decade. Sexuality became central to these investigations, not—as psychoanalysis would have it—as a key to the individual psyche, but as a means of flight from the inevitable "productive" boredom of monogamous hetero life. Gay sex and hippie "free-love" offered new, nonprivatized forms of sexuality. Liberated sexuality was more than a conduit to personal freedom: it was a means of disrupting the social order, overturning the power dynamic at the heart of the nuclear family and forging new forms of alliances. What would happen if people took sex less seriously?

Numerous publications—from Larry Flint's *Screw* to France's elite philosophical journal *Recherches*—explored the implications of polyphonous sexuality.

But perhaps the most daring (and entertaining) cultural intervention to emerge during these years was *Suck—The First European Sex Paper.*

Founded in London in 1969 by veteran underground publishers Jim Haynes and Bill Levy together with activist writers Heathcote Williams and Germaine Greer and the model Jean Shrimpton, *Suck* celebrated hippie free love and gay and lesbian sexuality. Sex was fun, sex was an integral part of cultural currency. The first editorial board meeting took place in the offices of London's staid *Transatlantic Review*, and as *Suck* lore has it, at some point Williams and Shrimpton excused themselves to have sex in the adjoining room. "Later," Jim Haynes would wryly recall, "I looked back on this meeting as our first mistake. We should all five have made love together." The magazine was banned in the UK before the first issue circulated. Haynes promptly shifted production to Amsterdam, enlisting his Dutch friend Willem De Ridder—creator of *Image Storm,* a magazine inspired by Fluxus and confluent with Williams' inspired exposure of "media burn" in his play *AC/DC*—as co-publisher.

Over the next five years, *Suck* intermittently published eight issues, produced in various cities in Europe and the US in short intense periods when the group lived together. In 1970 and 1971, *Suck* staged the Wet Dream Film Festival of banned erotic and pornographic films in Amsterdam and later published a book—*Wet Dreams: Films and Adventures*—to commemorate the two festivals. "Everyone was lovely," Jim Haynes recalled in his 1984 autobiography, *Thanks for Coming!* "Suddenly the vision of everyone Coming Together could only be physical … no longer intellectual. The sex politics of Reich, the belief of Auden that we must love one another or die, the holy orgiastics of Willie Blake, God's Rake, had to burst through… *Suck* was a display of pantheistic and revolutionary *schtupping*. You cannot fuck everyone in the world, but at least you can try."

Why is it that to this day every sexual libertarian movement in history is viewed with a wink, if not a chastising sneer? In her diminishing biography of Havelock Ellis, the 19th century's premiere sexologist, renaissance mind, and utopian pioneer, the psychoanalyst Phyllis Grosskurth concludes that Ellis' choice of a nonmonogamous marriage to Edith Ellis, a bisexual social theorist and writer, proves only that Havelock "simply could not stand the intimacy of a married relationship." Moreover, she continues, he was probably impotent!

In our era, sex in itself is no longer taboo or shocking. American porn outgrosses professional sports at $12 billion a year. But for an otherwise credible thinker to disclose the fact of his or her own nonmonogamous life—to propose new models of sexuality while using his or her own life as an example—is professional suicide. Cultural critic Laura

Kipnis avoided the first person in *Against Love*, her 2003 polemic on monogamy and its discontents to (perhaps) shield the work from this kind of first-degree ridicule.

And yet it's almost impossible to talk about sexuality without being implicated. We are all sexual beings, but to put oneself in the equation is to invite scorn and dismissal. *Suck* faced this dilemma head-on in a spirit of serious play with confrontational humor. *Total disclosure*. Every debate led back to the political and emotional lives of its founders. As Germaine Greer would write later: "My reason for joining the editorial board was that we needed an antidote to the exploitative pornography of papers like *Screw* and *Hustler*. I tried to insist on using male bodies as often as female, invading the privacy of the editors, naming names in sex news and developing a new kind of erotic art."

"Suck wipes out the energy fetishism of Romance and Privacy... Suck smashes Sexual Elitism with photos of old people making it beautifully... Suck destroys jealousy... Suck is crucial shit," Heathcote Williams declared in the *Suck* manifesto.

The editors of *Suck* magazine routinely invaded their own and each other's privacy, often to brilliant effect. They all appeared nude in the magazine. They commented freely on their sexual encounters, including—even especially—those with each other. This practice of creating an alternative culture while at the same time reporting on it had already begun in the mid-1960s. When Jim Haynes founded London's underground *International Times* in 1966, "the policy of the paper was that while we would report the news, it was far more interesting to *make* news—to create events for the underground community, give those events a great deal of advance publicity and then report on them after they happened." In this way, the publication itself becomes just one part of a larger cultural work. Somewhat informed by 20th century avant-gardes like Situationism and Fluxus, *IT* and *Suck* introduced high-art ethos and strategies to a non-art-world audience who, with no particular stakes in the cultural game, randomly sampled ideas and made them bigger and messier. The proliferation of the underground press during an era with so few media sources allowed *Suck* to create a sensational impact with meager financial resources. Cultural intervention was cheap—or in another sense, very costly, because it required a total commitment of one's own time and energy.

No one exercised this method more boldly than Germaine Greer. Attaining instant celebrity when her 1970 book *The Female Eunuch* appeared on the cusp of the international feminist movement, she pointedly refused the "exceptional woman" status that, until then, was bestowed on a handful of prominent intellectual women. Hannah Arendt and Mary McCarthy declined to align themselves with the feminist movement, and for good reason. Greer, on the other hand, sought total democracy: "I'm sick of being treated differently because I have more intellectual credentials than a girl who sleeps around without the credentials," she asserted in a 1971 *Evergreen* magazine interview. "My feeling is, if there is a whore in the world, let them call me a whore."

I am Spartacus. Like Carolee Schneeman and Hannah Wilke, Greer used her own body as a site of gender polemics. In *Suck #6*, she proposed an end to monogamy (a position she never recanted) as a feminist strategy, less for the sake of variety than as a means to free women from sexual jealousy and the idea of their own bodies as quickly devalued, diminishing capital. "Ideally," she wrote, "you've got to get to the stage where you could really ball everyone— the fat, the blind, the foolish, the impotent, the dishonest… Everything we do is erotic… People despise their sexuality so much."

Deliberately shunning soft porn's sexual-fantasy romance aesthetic, *Suck*'s editors favored contributions written in the first person. From the first issue on, the magazine strategically mixed amateur contributions with writings by some of the great minds of the 20th century. Texts by William S. Burroughs, Maurice Girodias, Jean-Jacques Lebel, Roland Topor, and Brion Gysin appeared alongside musings from readers like Mrs. A.R. of London, who observed: "Your lovely name *Suck*… is proving to men and showing women that their cunts no longer have to be dominated by a hard-thrusting cock."

Sexual practices were described matter-of-factly. In "Ass Fucking Can Be a Lot of Fun," one female contributor explained: "The first time I was fucked in the ass it didn't turn me off. The guy asked me how it felt and I said it was like going to the bathroom backwards. Sometimes I really dig it and sometimes I don't. It's different each time. What angers me is to be told that it is debasing to me as a woman. My body is my own… No one can tell me what to do with my ass." Compared with Toni Bentley's 2004 haute chick-lit erotic memoir *The Surrender* on the same practice—"I see his cock as a therapeutic instrument… He fucks me into my femininity"—the *Suck* essay seems not only refreshing but also brilliant in its attempt to wrest female sexuality from the realm of confession and psychoanalysis.

Total disclosure about all forms of experience demystified sex acts that, while practiced widely, were still seen as taboo or dirty. This kind of disclosure also preempted any attempt to mythologize the magazine's more famous founders. Ideas were always in motion together with sucking and fucking, and no one took him or herself terribly seriously. *Suck*'s writers and editors argued constantly and publicly among themselves in the paper; there was never any "last word." While in our decade the "personal" has become so debased by its confessional-therapeutic connotations that numerous artists choose to anonymize their production, *Suck*'s authors viewed disclosure not as personal narcissism but as a means of escaping the limits of "self." Liberated sexuality was an exchange of information: "Confrontation," as Greer writes in *Wet Dreams*, "is political awareness."

Conversely in Paris, where it all began, the immediate cultural repercussions of May '68 were initially drawn in narrower terms. The New Left continued its critique of institutions, mostly targeting the university where its members had already received tenure. For years, before their brief romance with Maoism, the influential Tel Quel group's tepid response to the luminous notion that the personal is political was to simply conflate Marxism and psychoanalysis. It was not until 1971, when gay activists and lesbian feminists joined to form the Front Homosexuel d'Action Revolutionnaire (FHAR, meaning Homosexual Front for Revolutionary Action), that sexuality and daily life were seen as the locus of politics. In an April 1971 manifesto published in the leftist newspaper *Tout!* the group outrageously proclaimed:

> *We are more than 343 sluts*
> *We have been buggered by Arabs*
> *We are proud of it and we will do it again*

Supported by Jean-Paul Sartre, who was then the Director of Publications of *Tout!*, FHAR's activities drew the attention of Félix Guattari, who had just finished writing *Anti-Oedipus* with Gilles Deleuze. Wasn't FHAR's demand for visibility and their scathing contempt for family life, and the received ideas of the New Left a live demonstration of the theories of social deterritorialization he and Deleuze sought to elaborate? "Making love," they famously wrote in *Anti-Oedipus*, "is not just becoming as one, or even two, but becoming as a hundred thousand." Or, as one of FHAR's slogans put it: *Workers of the World, Fondle Yourselves!*

In March 1973, Guatarri joined with members of FHAR to coedit a special issue of *Recherches*, the house journal of the government-funded Center for Institutional Study, Research, and Training, which he then codirected. Titled "Three Billion Perverts: The Great Encyclopedia of Homosexualities," the magazine had profound intellectual and legal repercussions. Within a month issues of the magazine were seized by police and destroyed. Nevertheless, a handful of copies of this extraordinary document continue to circulate. Beyond the amusing diversion of Guattari's trial (which he played to the Kafkaesque hilt, questioning the very notion of representation), "Three Billion Perverts" was a landmark in French cultural politics. The normally staid academic compendium of scholarly articles was transformed into a 'zine with cartoons and snapshots, personal testimony, pornographic drawings, and diary excerpts presented alongside theoretical essays. Numerous revered

French intellectuals contributed work to "Three Billion Perverts," but because the pieces were presented anonymously, no one will ever be sure if the drawing of a penis wrapped in a turban was made by Jean-Paul Sartre, Michel Foucault, Fanny Deleuze, Jean Genet, Guy Hocquenghem, or one of the less well-known contributors whose names appeared on the masthead.

In an unsigned introduction, Guattari argued that homosexuality could no longer be seen within sociology's methodological framework. "It's not enough to merely 'give the subject a voice,'" he wrote. "We must create the conditions that make this possible." Not only must homosexuality be depathologized; but gay rights organizations should avoid mimicking heterosexual values in their bid for civil rights. In 1974, Guattari perceived the trend among gay rights organizations to "normalize" homosexuality by replicating nuclear heterosexual "family values." "May '68 taught us to read the writing on the walls," he concluded, "and since then we have started to decipher the graffiti in prisons, asylums, and now, public toilets."

This was devastating. "Three Billion Perverts" was light years beyond the New Left's bland institutional critique. In one sentence, Guattari succeeded in equating one of France's most revered intellectual journals with a urinal.

"On the boat, people are SUCKING and FUCKING, coming together as closer nonseparate objects...

a float… learning more about themselves in time-space and orgasms," the artist Mel Clay wrote in Suck's *Wet Dreams* book.

Thirty-five years later, much as Guattari had predicted, homosexuality has been largely absorbed into the mainstream so long as it mirrors heterosexual life. The radical implications of gay lifestyles discussed by Tony Duvert, Guy Hocquenghem, Michel Foucault, and others during that era remain marginal. The level of scorn that greeted Andrea Fraser's fairly innocuous 2003 video work *Untitled* (in which the artist video-tapes herself having sex with a collector who has agreed to purchase the work for $20,000) through-out the art world proves just how far mores have shifted since the 1970s. Discourse around Fraser's work centered on questions like: How Many Hours A Day Does She Spend Working Out? and Is She A Narcissist? In this climate, endeavors like *Suck* and "Three Billion Perverts" seem newly important. As Greer wrote in *The Whole Woman*, her 1999 sequel to *The Female Eunuch*, "In 1970 the [women's] movement was called 'Women's Liberation' or, contemptuously, 'Women's Lib.' When the name 'Libbers' was dropped for 'Feminists' we were all relieved. What none of us noticed was that the ideal of liberation was fading out with the word."

## 5

DETOUR

February 8, 2008: I'm in "quiet" Van #1 of the 2008 Sex Workers Art Show and it isn't *that* quiet—Keva, Erin, and Krylon are playing some kind of *Guess That Song* game based on the hits of 2002, the year they all finished high school—but it's definitely more quiet than Van #2, which since the second week of the tour established itself as the mobile party. This isn't to say Van #2 is drinking or drugging. Unlike the artists on previous tours, none of us has trouble abiding by Tara's "no drugs in the van" rule. No one here drinks. No one even smokes. On the rare days we have a few hours off, half of the group holds AA meetings.

We're driving up 95 North to New York. Up front, Tara's on the phone with The Zipper Theater, the venue. Tonight's 10 p.m. show is sold out and she's trying to get them to add a second show at midnight. Last night we did two shows in DC. The tour started more than three weeks ago in Portland and since then, we've been zigzagging across the US. Tomorrow the vans will head west, then north, then east, and then west. By the end of the month we'll be in Kentucky. With gas at $3.50 a gallon, the tour isn't a lucrative proposition. We stay in 5-star hotels but sleep four to a room. Unless we miss shows we'll each leave the tour with $3200. For some of us, this is a lot; for others, very little. Except in my case (I'm at least two decades older than the other artists) the difference is largely determined by who is, or is not, still doing sex work.

Keva Lee is a social worker and dominatrix. Lorelei Lei is a student and porn star. The writer/performer Kirk Read works part-time as an escort, part-time as a counselor at a clinic for Bay Area sex workers. Krylon Superstar works as a florist. I own apartments (is this the fate of every old whore?) and am teaching at UC San Diego. Dirty Martini and World Famous Bob are celebrities on the New Burlesque circuit, but in 2008 "New Burlesque" inhabits the fringe of the art world. Like other performance artists in New York without family support, their economic existence is marginal. After the feverish flu that swept through the vans in Week #2, those of us who could afford it began buying plane tickets to avoid the really long hauls. Alert to the potential divisiveness of this class gap, Tara made a new rule: *Everyone on the tour will stay with the vans.* (Still, I'm still allowed to fly back every two weeks to keep my job in San Diego.)

Tara Perkins—founder, creative director, and mastermind of the Sex Workers' Art Tour—is like the Mother Jones of 21st century whoredom. Brilliant and completely self-educated, Perkins spent her youth waitressing in the Northwest before becoming the paid companion of an older lesbian, a situation she recalls with some ambivalence but which nevertheless gave her time to pursue various interests. She is also one of the most winning and capable people I've ever met. Every night, she strides onstage in a pair of 5" silver Manolos, pre-Raphaelite red Kool-Aid hair flaming, and tells the youth of America's elite colleges what the minimum wage is: "5.65! And (you do the math) at $12 billion a year, the American porn industry outgrosses professional sports. But," she adds with a smile, "I won't bore you with politics. You all came to see naked ladies!"

"Really," she told me one night over a glass of red wine, "I'm not doing the show to valorize sex work. We all know what *that's* about. The show is a way to bring people together, and maybe open their eyes a little bit to other issues. The sex stuff is good because it gets people out. I mean, would anyone come if I did an art show with fast-food workers?"

This will be the last year of the Sex Workers Art Show. Beth Ditto has already hired Tara to manage The Gossip. In a week, she'll jump tour to fly to

London. Sony will send a limo to pick her up from our show in Connecticut and she'll discover her wallet and passport were stolen at last night's dive bar but Sony will get her a new one in hours. Three days later, she'll be back for the show in Ann Arbor.

It's gray, slushy, and cold outside the van windows. Kirk Read is wearing a hoodie and a pair of felt slippers he packs for the van. World Famous Bob (Your Dream Girl Come True!) has on a blue suede winter coat over sweat pants. Tonight she'll be wearing a skin-tight sequined dress over her extravagant six-foot frame and glittery butterfly eyelashes, regaling the crowd with the story of how she, a runaway farm girl from a small town in the San Joaquin Valley, became a taxi-dancer ("Kids," she will wink, "do you know what that is?") in a seedy Los Angeles bar. She'll finish taking her clothes off and stand, arms stretched under a spotlight while orchestral music swells, reciting a homily—"Remember, whatever it is you think you want, you probably already have it"—which will feel suddenly utterly true and triumphant. I've seen Bob do this act at least 20 times and while (unlike some of the other performers) her script is completely set, each night she stretches the shape of it in a new way so it always feels fresh and occasional. Watching her, I think of Brecht's direction to actors: "Wear your character like a jumpsuit. Do not ever forget you're in front of an audience."

And isn't her act a very pure form of the V-effect, which, unlike some drearier forays into that genre, never forgets that the primary job of an actor is to be *entertaining*? When Erin Markey's head mike fell off one night during her pole dance, Bob told her, "Oh honey. Whatever happens out there, you've just got to find some way to use it."

Krylon Superstar's act, on the other hand, is all process. A tall black gay man in his late 20s, Krylon wears women's clothes in the show but makes no attempt to impersonate a real woman. His character—wearing a ratty magenta wig and a white tutu—evokes the outer femme reaches of what is otherwise masculine. During the first few shows Krylon's act—that ends with him wallowing in a small kiddie pool after awkwardly stripping—seemed unformed and confusing. Five days into the tour, we did a show in his hometown San Diego, where some of his friends who'd signed up for the National Guard were awaiting deployment. It occurred to him to sing an original song during his strip about the war in Iraq, a capella. It brought down the house. Later, he had Rocco the techie play a recording of Kate Smith's *God Bless America* while he rolls around nude in the pool coating himself with glitter. At first sight, this juxtaposition was bracingly shocking, but as the song and the wallowing went on, it became something else, more disturbing. Later, he wrote the words FUCK BUSH on a strip of duct tape that he put on his chest and revealed midway through the strip. Still later, he had Rocco walk onstage midway through *God Bless America*, insert a Fourth-of-July sparkler up his ass and ignite it. As time goes on, the antiwar theme will become more elaborate, but by the time we get to Ann Arbor he'll drop the song altogether. He will be bored with it.

Every day in the van is the same. We're never fully awake for the 9 or 10 a.m. departure—after speaking to audience members, selling merch, striking and loading, we rarely get back to the hotel before 2 or 3 in the morning. For 8 or 9 hours we're cocooned on the road, not fully alert until show time. All this time spent dragging the body around for the 10 or 15 minutes we each spend performing! The tour feels like a tour-of-duty. The tour posters say, *New Whore Order*. We're all in the live-art army, giving thousands of people across the US a reason to leave their houses and dorm rooms to sit in a theater together. And who could say it's not worth it? My credentials for joining the tour are marginal. It's been more than two decades since I worked as a topless dancer. Each time I get up to read the piece I wrote for the tour—a chronicle of time spent in New York's pre-AIDS hustle bars—I'm afraid the full houses will bolt, finding these observations too flinty and literary. But they don't, and it's exhilarating. Where else except, perhaps, pre-glasnost Russia or

Poland could a writer of literary fiction read to standing-room only crowds of 600 people?

Since Tara appeared on Fox News last week to be pilloried by Laura Ingraham, her phone hasn't stopped ringing. We still don't know where we'll be sleeping tonight after the (now confirmed) late show. Finally around 4 when we enter New Jersey she stops taking calls and begins one of her preshow rituals: using her Blackberry to log on to Hotwire and find the best last-minute deal for the night's accommodations.

"Are you *for* or *against* sex work?" American youth wants to know, from Harvard to Duke to UC Davis. The question strikes all of us in the vans as absurd. It's like asking if someone is "for" or "against" global capitalism. Since we left San Francisco—where we were blessed by a transgendered warlock onstage at the Victoria Theater—controversy has followed the vans across the US. The San Diego City Council passed an ordinance in our honor, prohibiting live performance in downtown storefronts. The promoters responded by moving the venue from a lesbian-owned adult toy store to a gay bar outside of town. UCLA cancelled six hours before show time and paid us *not* to perform. But it wasn't until we pulled into historic Williamsburg, Virginia (Cradle of Our Nation's History) to perform at the College of William and Mary that shit hit the fan big time.

For weeks, grassroots right-wing organizations had been pressuring now-former Gene Nichol, to cancel the show. "A disturbing 'art' show is making its way to America's college campuses," blogged CitizenLink. "Prostitutes and pornographers are referred to as 'artists' and 'geniuses.'" Education Department professor John Foubert warned that "the Sex Workers' Art Show is likely to bring increased sexual aggression" to the community because "exposing people, particularly men, to pornography, makes them more likely to commit sexual assault." Why should the "free speech of pornographers and pimps" be protected, the local press asked. "Tit torture, ball-crushing whip-yielding, and works like *I Love Dick* only bring shame to our campus." "They're all pigs with lipstick!" opined one columnist. Republican State Assembly Representative Brenda Pogue wrote to Nichol requesting he cancel the show. "Williamsburg is a destination that families come to from across the nation and learn of our Nation's founding. A show of this nature violates a standard of decency citizens of this area uphold and wish to maintain…" Virginia State Attorney General Bob McDonnell rewrote a statute exempting college campuses from the state's obscenity laws. But Nichol stood firm. An avowed moderate, in this climate he was beginning to look like Nelson Mandela: "The First Amendment and the defining traditions of openness that sustain universities are hallmarks of academic inquiry and freedom. It is the speech we disdain that often puts these principles to the test."

Tara was forced to sign a new contract that forbade all recording, the sale of tour merchandise, or partial nudity. Each of the 1000 attendees at the two sold-out performances would have to be carded. No one under age 21 would be allowed into the auditorium.

When we arrived at the college we walked single file through a gauntlet of Fox News and local TV reporters. Christian protestors who followed us for the Southern leg of the tour staged a prayer vigil. The shows were a triumph. Eight days later, Nichol was fired.

We drove through Colonial Williamsburg on the way from the hotel to the venue… a cluster of quaint, squat 18th century houses restored as an "authentic" colonial century village… whites and anomalous blacks costumed as blacksmiths and chandlers in breeches and bonnets conducted their pantomime business. I sat next to Lorelei Lei who, in the same year, received both the Bishop Award for Best Younger Poet and AdultCon's award for Best Tit Torture Actress. Lorelei, 27, carried a pink Hello Kitty backpack and wore hot pants and short ruffled skirts with knee socks throughout the deep Northeast winter. A well-known advocate of the sex-positive power of porn, her writings reveal something darker.

As we drove through the streets, Lorelei leaned towards the window with her video camera and I saw the town through her eyes. We were being run out of Virginia as witches.

## 6

## DESCRIPTION OVER PLOT

My first reaction to seeing Moyra Davey's *32 Photographs from Paris* (2009) at her Murray Guy show was: excitement. It felt so subversive, seeing these poster-sized prints installed side-by-side in the main room of this large Chelsea gallery. Davey had initially sent them as oversized postcards to friends in New York and Canada while she was in Paris and then borrowed them back for the show. They'd been folded and stamped and sent through the mail, and you could barely make out the stations and dates on the French postmarks.

I can't remember if the prints were taped to the wall (they were probably not), but it *felt* like it. With a comfortable couch placed in front of a monitor (installed in a box that vaguely evoked an old-fashioned television) playing a loop of her 2009 videotape *My Necropolis*, Davey had somehow evoked—in the chill of a commercial gallery—the feeling of energized hominess captured in hundreds of earlier works shot over two decades in her family's New York apartments. Though there may be dust under the *Bed* (2003) or appliances stacked on top of the *Fridge* (2003), these images neither attempt—as many art installations did in the late 1990s—to fabulate mess or document squalor. They simply depict the texture of spaces fully inhabited. Davey is highly attuned to how our perception of images is determined by where and how they are exhibited. As she writes in her 2007 essay "Notes on Photography and Accident":

*It's becoming clear to me that … accident is to be located outside the frame somehow, in the way we apprehend images. I shun the formal encounter via the institutions of galleries and museums, and gravitate to books and journals.*

If you want to control the outcome, control the process.

I didn't immediately connect the Murray Guy installation to the thoughtful critique of highly staged large-scale digital prints ("stilt coupled by bloat," as Davey put it) that she pursued in that essay, but the room felt like a rejoinder to the boredom evinced by the images of 21st century crowds and architectural surfaces produced by Andreas Gursky and legions of imitators on the cusp of the millennium.

As cultural theorist Franco Berardi observes in *The Soul at Work*, "We renew our affection for work because economic survival becomes more difficult and daily life becomes lonely and tedious: metropolitan life becomes so sad that we might as well sell it for money." Or as Davey herself writes:

*Many of the pictures produced by [digital enhancement] are fundamentally no different from the gaudy mid-nineteenth-century pictorialist tableaux of Henry Peach Robinson and F. Holland Day… the art world at its most absurd: Mount Rushmore-scale pieties, dwarfed only by the deafening ka-ching of the cash register.*

Davey's Paris—with its shadowy rooms and café crèmes, shredded maps, thick coats of paint on exterior doorways and overgrown ancient cemeteries—is a place I'd still want to visit. As in hundreds of earlier images, though I'm thinking especially of *Simcha Buttons* (1996) and *Laura Nyro* (2003), Davey's shots of urban everyday objects in France acquire some of their glamour through her use of deep viscous saturations of color. The things in her Paris pictures—café table tops, empty glasses, a red leather chair, an ashtray—look like shiny bubbles of plastic jewelry, like the translucent jellybean drops left on one of the Paris gravesites she filmed.

The components of Davey's Paris constellation of work—which includes *32 Photographs From Paris, My Necropolis*, an underlined Xeroxed page from one of Walter Benjamin's letters to Gerhard Scholem, and "Index Cards" (2008–2009), the latter being Davey's extraordinary written meditation on illness, sleep, speed, mortality, and adaptation that narrates and guides the rest of the project—are densely connected by internal references and almost magical correspondences. Maps, clocks, gravesites, and books recur in the photographs, the *Necropolis* video, and the fragments of 20th century essays and novels the artist collects and responds to in acute real-time writing. Together, the writing and visual work form a system in which (as in life) meaning occurs through accretion. But I didn't know that when I stumbled into the Murray Guy show last December. I just thought: this person is doing something really important. "Moyra Davey is amazing!" someone named Erik wrote on the Carefully Aimed Darts blog after seeing the show. And the photos were gorgeous.

Davey's auto-fiction videotape *50 Minutes* (2005) begins with the artist considering her relation to the shifting contents of her refrigerator:

*A well-stocked fridge always triggers a certain atavistic, metabolic anxiety, like that of the Neanderthal after the kill, faced with the task of needing to either ingest or preserve a massive abundance of food before spoilage sets in.*

*I get an unmistakable pleasure out of seeing… [long pause; narrator again forgets her lines; off-screen voice tells her to wait five seconds and start over] the contents of the fridge diminish, out of seeing the spaces between the food items get larger and better defined… That is my aim with the fridge: to be able to open it and see as much of its clean, white, empty walls as possible.*

Eventually she will arrive at her subject: the psychoanalysis she underwent for five and a half years paid for mostly with her own time. (The analyst charged her $8 per session providing she saw him five days a week to fulfill the conditions of his Psychoanalytic Institute internship.) Davey is wryly ambivalent about the analysis and her digressive narration follows the form of an analysand's hour. The tape's visual content is largely illustrational. Moving pictures keep us in place watching the tape in a gallery, but Davey's voice is clearly what's driving the work. The thrill is all in the story. The primary visuals—the fridge, the apartment interiors—reprise a body of photographs she took two years prior.

The text/image configuration in *50 Minutes* suggests a template for Davey's thought process in two ways that seem important. First, the interrelation of elements: a written narrative, a videotape that offers an excursion into the physical world, and the still photographs form a rough constellation that she will elaborate further in Paris. In both bodies of work, Davey offers herself as protagonist pursuing a set of ideas in multiple forms. Like the Bernadette Corporation, Davey's work is a kind of gestural poetry—an ability to respond to the present—that can be expressed in various media. Second, she is a collector, but what she collects are her encounters with things. Davey's *dérives* through the shabby detritus of urban and everyday life insert the *psycho* in psycho-geography. While the Situationist forays into Europe's mid-century neighborhoods were in fact rather programmatic and dry, Davey has always offered herself as a fully present, human respondent. In her 2007 essay "Notes on Photography and Accident," she writes longingly about transforma-tion, the intangible thing that (she quotes Garry Winogrand) "makes a picture alive and not dead." Picking some film up from the lab, she laments, "no transformation … I may as well admit it, I'm blocked." The essay conjures a powerful nostalgia for the ethos of transformation and accident that she sees as an antidote to the "stilt coupled with bloat" that has come to define contemporary photography. Yet the "transformation" that takes place within Davey's remarkable constellations is no accident. It is the result of accretion, the arrangement of images, text, and lived experience that she collects over time.

In July 2006 Davey was diagnosed with multiple sclerosis, a degenerative disease that results in loss of vision, muscle weakness and spasms, depression, speech problems, and acute pain. Though this diagnosis is not disclosed until the last page of "Notes on Photography and Accident," Davey's urgent need to adapt to a weakened condition informs her brilliant discussion of practice in the essay. She's blocked. She's exhausted. The combination of illness and medications lead her to spend a great deal of time in bed, where she sits writing. Lulled by fatigue, she considers ceasing production completely—the lure to just simply *be*. Or else: she needs to arrive at a new way of working. On the very first page she decides, "I want to make some photographs, but I want them to take seed in words."

While Davey had always been a prodigious reader—her 2003 essay-length book, *The Problem of Reading*, is a phenomenological meditation on the various ways one might experience the printed word—she decides in her "Notes" essay to actively use writing and reading as part of her practice. That is, she decides to write as a writer. Opening John Cage's *Notations* at random, she reads, *I mix chance and choice somewhat scandalously*, and then writes, "I copy this phrase into a notebook, a perfect encapsulation of my own desire for contingency within a structure. I decide to allow chance elements, the *flânerie*, as it were, of daily life, to find their way into this essay." (Asked once if his cut-ups were "truly" random, the writer William S. Burroughs replied, "Yes, but it's *my* random.")

Mid-essay, Davey receives her first Interferon injection and ventures out of the house. "Picture of dust motes in sunlight after shaking out bedspread; picture of large weed growing by the West Side

Highway. I've broken the ice, am taking pictures again. I risk something, but what?"

That same weed (I imagine) stars in the opening scene of *My Necropolis*. For some reason, the shot stands out. Viewing the tape before reading her "Accident" essay, I write in my notebook: "The color of grass in Washington Heights at the end of a wet summer … a movement outward. The view of the dead she shoots through a window and the 32 faux-tourist photos she sends through the mail to her friends are both ways of traveling out: in the first case, she/the artist is traveling towards something—but in the second, she/through the object is traveling also, to friends."

Clocks—a recurring icon in the Paris work—make their first appearance in "Notes on Photography and Accident." Combing through Walter Benjamin's "A Short History of Photography" and Roland Barthes' *Camera Lucida*, she gets—

**Lost**

*As I'm writing I start to remember, or think I remember, reading that Benjamin (or was it Barthes?) wrote about clocks in photographs, the idea of a picture recording the exact moment of its taking. I flip through books, hoping I've made a mark. But the thing I was looking to find remains lost. I feel unlucky.*

and at the end of the essay she—

**Notes**

*I still haven't come across that lost reference to clocks. I did, however, begin to read Walter Benjamin's correspondence, and in a letter to Gershom Scholem... he describes his study, a room with a panoramic view from which he can see the ice-skating rinks, as well as a clock: "as time goes by, it is especially this clock that becomes a luxury it is difficult to do without." Benjamin also tells Scholem: "I now write only while lying down."*

**Scenes of a heightened struggle for existence... books... (study)... I now write only while lying down... sofa... l'atelier qui chante et qui bavarde... As time goes by, it is especially this clock that becomes a luxury that it is difficult to do without... piano**

> —Words underlined by Moyra Davey in the
> Walter Benjamin letter to Gershom Scholem

Davey's text "Index Cards" begins with a diary entry dated December 20, 2007. At that moment, "Notes on Photography and Accident" is about to be published in *Long Life Cool White*, the book produced as part of her retrospective at Harvard's Fogg Art Museum the following April. Together, the two texts comprise a kind of serial novel. But in "Index Cards," Davey begins with a mandate:

*To have been driven all one's life by some poorly understood mechanism in one's body and then be asked to cut the speed by a half or two-thirds is asking a great deal. I am trying to find a new way to work.*

Though Davey won't leave for Paris until late August, she has already decided to produce a project "rooted in travel, linked by three cemeteries in three cities in three moments in time." Her family's Washington Heights apartment overlooks an old graveyard and she has a strong memory of stumbling into a New Orleans cemetery while traveling two decades before: "little necropolises in blinding white sunlight and intense, nearly unbearable heat." While the associations between clocks, cemeteries, illness, and mortality are too glaringly obvious to be overlooked, the cemeteries she tapes and photographs seem more like collections of statuary, a meeting place between the living and dead. Like the textual sources she draws from in "Index Cards"—works by Benjamin, Charles Baudelaire, Jane Bowles, Bruno Schulz, and Virginia Woolf—their stately repose belongs to past centuries. On April 25, "It's a warm spring day, the cemetery is now almost obscured by soft green yellow and red bursts of leaves."

I can't recall even one of my prematurely deceased contemporaries being interred in a cemetery. In death as in life, we are nomadic.

In June, Davey rereads the Walter Benjamin letter: "Walter Benjamin writes to his friend Gershom Scholem that his 2,000 books have arrived, and that he now writes only while lying down. From his study he has a panoramic view of the ice-skating rinks, Schramm Lake and a clock. He calls the scene 'almost *l'atelier qui chante et qui bavarde.*'" This cryptic letter becomes the starting point for her work about writing, illness, sleep, and the view from the window. Baudelaire, Woolf, Aldo Rossi, and Dennis Potter, she finds, have all described supine or convalescent views of clouds, patches of blue sky, blossoms, or crowds seen with the innocence of children. "The look of the world altered by illness. … What do we do when the part of us that could go 'all out' is no longer available?"

On July 5, Davey suffers "two days of hell following Cymbalta when I thought I was dying," but three weeks later she goes out and begins shooting film in the graveyard across from her house. "Finally: experience of being in the cemetery, almost deafening chant of cicadas and crows … 28 July. Back to the cemetery 3rd time: it is *L'atelier qui chante et qui bavarde.* I am working again. I am alive."

At the time of Benjamin's letter—December 20, 1931—Sholem is living in Palestine and Benjamin himself has recently moved into his own Berlin apartment. Recently divorced, age 39, his life to that point had been wildly nomadic. The move to the Schramm Lake apartment—also described somewhat in one of his signature essays "Unpacking My Library"— offered a promise of permanence that never arrived. That April he'd leave on an extended trip to Ibiza.

Less than a year after that he'd leave Berlin permanently, finding "the German atmosphere in which you first look at people's lapels [for Nazi insignia] and after that do not want to look them in the face anymore," completely unbearable. A wistful retrospective knowledge of fate breathes through the letter… yet this isn't the aspect Davey grabs hold of. She's drawn to the clock and the couch. In her state of health, "Now I must close eyes, sleep, breathe."

In August, Davey leaves for Paris with Jason Simon, her partner, and their son Barney to begin a ten-month residency at Cité Internationale des Arts in the Marais. As well as shooting the Paris photographs and *My Necropolis*, she is preparing a talk that she'll give at the Dia Foundation on Louise Bourgeois. She writes, "I am trying to find a new way to work," and in Paris correspondences between these various projects begin to abound. Researching her talk, Davey counterpoises Bourgeois with Marguerite Duras and the way that both artists conflate domestic interiors with the maternal. Videotaping *My Necropolis* in the Montparnasse cemetery, her camera moves smoothly over pots of browned roses on Duras' grave. Walking through the Passage Jouffroy and its gallery of shops soon after arriving, she observes big broken clocks, and one of the *32 Photographs from Paris* depicts dozens of old clocks seen through a plate-glass store window in a Benjamin-esque arcade. "What would it look like," she wonders, "to pry open the fist of Paris? Pleasure of maps, figuring out where I have been and where I will go." She fights off sleep, she can't sleep, she combs books for other writers' notations of sleep, she feels "sleep as the weight of gravity weighing me down," and remembers the words *She Is Not Dead But Sleepeth* engraved on a cross in the Washington Heights cemetery that appears in the first scene of *My Necropolis.*

Sampled text from the Benjamin letter becomes a refrain as Davey walks with her camera through the Paris cemeteries. *What does Benjamin mean when he mentions the clock*, she'll ask Jason and Barney and a handful of friends in the second part of *My Necropolis.*

"To call clocks a luxury is somewhat odd, because anything that reminds you of the passage of time would be quite the opposite. Of a luxury," the writer Alison Strayer deadpans.

Simon (who appeared as a kind of wisecracking sage in Davey's 1990 video *Hell Notes*) picks up on Benjamin's wit. Living in horrible circumstances, broke and unable to even purchase a desk, Benjamin is, according to Simon, making a joke: "Everything he sees through the window is an appointment of luxury that comes with the rent." But it's Simon and Davey's 11 year-old son Barney who comes closest to voicing the most obvious correspondence. Struggling to gather his thoughts, he says, "I think what he is trying to say is that time is something you should know. It can tell you if you're late, if you have time to kill. So what I think is, you should—to know something is better than not knowing it."

"You must write as if you're already dead," Davey writes in "Index Cards," quoting David Rieff who is in turn quoting Nadine Gordimer.

Walter Benjamin traveled to Moscow in the winter of 1926. Though he financed the trip by writing essays on cultural life in the world's first communist nation for Berlin periodicals, he was led by desire to see Asja Lācis, to whom his first book, *One Way Street*, was dedicated. But when he arrived, Benjamin found her unavailable. Hospitalized for a mysterious illness throughout most of his stay, she was otherwise living with Bernhard Reich, a theater director who was also a close friend of Benjamin's. The three friends spent many evenings together at Lācis' bedside eating halvah and playing dominos— evenings described in the diaries as being more pleasant than awkward. Sometimes Reich and Benjamin went to the theater together. Reich volunteered as his tour guide, introducing him to people from all walks of communist life, from Bertolt Brecht to a factory forewoman to an army general. Only twice during the six week sojourn does Benjamin go out with Asja. Descriptions of days crammed with activity are punctuated with passing remarks like, "I shall not see Asja today." Towards the end of the stay he observes, "We are rarely alone together." A feeling of heartbreak courses beneath his engaging descriptions of Leninist Moscow, yet the diary isn't *about* heartbreak.

Rather, it is informed by heartbreak. When Lacsis stands him up for a date he records this and then goes on to describe St. Basil's Cathedral, the Moscow arcades, wooden toys, the political histories of new acquaintances, and the "beautiful view of the long string of lights" on a boulevard. Grief—like hashish—can be sampled as an exquisitely potent intoxicant.

Similarly, Davey's writing is informed by illness but it isn't about *illness*. Life, as Deleuze once observed, isn't personal. Davey offers herself as protagonist to lead us towards recognitions that arise in a heightened intellectual/emotional state through *correspondence*. This is the aspect of Benjamin's work I see transmitted most clearly in her epic, heroic writing.

# 3. Matrix

7

LONG CENTURY

(For Kate Sennert)


*Thursday, August 7, '08 Punta Banda, Baja Mx …*

Quiet this summer on the peninsula—bad US economy plus weekly TV reports about car-jackings and kidnappings around the border. "You take your life in your hands going down there," someone told me. In fact it's much riskier here for the middle class Mexicans. Miguel Pabloff, who owns the campo I stay at, resigned from his post as mayor of Maneadero because of threats to his family, and there are regular kidnappings of local business owners. The guy who owns two Pemex gas stations in Maneadero was kidnapped and ransomed for $100,000… the owner of a local flower farm was kidnapped and murdered. "It's the Colombians," everyone says, "they are crazy." The common belief is that *Mexican* narcos would stop short of murder—mutilation, okay, but symbolic, not fatal. During last year's mayoral election in Rosarito, the incumbent's campaign manager was seized outside his office, bound, gagged and blindfolded, and finally released with his boss' nickname cut into his face with a razor.

Still, for us summer residents, it's blissfully quiet. There are a disturbing number of jellyfish washed up on the beach, but not as many as last year. And no red tide this year, no sting-rays.

Working on a novel about states of mind in underclass Bush America, I've been trying to learn more about psychoanalysis and therapy… the disciplines that, presumably, directly address daily forms of personal pain, numbness. I ask a few friends in this field what the new treatments are. Has anyone in the last 20 years undertaken transpositions of theory to clinical practice on the order of R.D. Laing's Kingsley Hall or Félix Guattari's Le Borde? The answers that come back are surprising. I'm referred to a website for Social Dreaming™, a group of mostly British psychoanalysts who contract "dream workshops" to large corporations. They claim to have successfully resolved a labor dispute at an Italian factory by having bosses and workers (they don't use these terms) pool their dreams. This seems truly innovative, a great advance on the Blackberry. From 40 hours a week to boundary-less wraparound time spent at work to the unconscious, although, as a more cynical friend points out, the unconscious has been pretty much drained of its content.

I've been watching Louis Malle's remarkable documentary *Phantom India* on DVD. Malle spent several months in India during 1969 with a small crew making this seven-hour film that was eventually shown on English television. It's a beautiful artifact of 20th century humanist generalism. Malle, then 35, resolved to keep an open mind about India, allowing impressions to float as he and his small crew moved around. Coming from the ideologically-steeped era of post-'68 Paris, Malle was not unaware of the political struggles then being waged between the Indian National and Communist parties, but as an outsider he was free to also consider the intractable beauty of folk religions whose meanings were reaffirmed in primitive daily routines. As an amateur ethnographer at the end of ethnography, he was aware of the battle of time taking place in front of his eyes between urban and rural. And yet, caste morphed into class, and this gently sanctified daily routine occured within a grossly exploitative framework. He drew no conclusions. I think about Malle's later life, his marriage to Candice Bergen, how naive this work might have seemed retrospectively. And yet, unrepeatable. (Later I read that towards the end of Malle's life, he considered this film his favorite.) *Phantom India* seems to be enjoying a small revival. A Michigan friend, a political activist, is screening it at a local community center this summer.

Jon Isaac tells me he's recording his music on cassette, not CD, because it's harder to upload. "One reason," he emails, "for the music industry's downfall is that music is too readily accessible. I remember seeing lines of people at record stores in the early '90s when an album came out b/c that was the only way you could hear the music."

## 8

INDELIBLE VIDEO

The complete ubiquity of video and other digital forms within contemporary art has rendered discussion about it, as a medium, obsolete. There is no longer anything singular about video. Images are everywhere. To attempt any one definition of video would be as meaningless as asking "what is contemporary art?" All art now is conceptual, defined by its stance in relation to other art and its place in the market. It would be more fruitful and interesting at this point to ask how an image transcends other images, or even more to the point: How can the market be used to do what art used to do?

Baudrillard describes the incursion of images into every sector of life. Striving for emptiness when it is already empty, visual art has become *transaesthetic*. Like pornography, art no longer exists because it is virtually everywhere. Naïve to complain that the market has vanquished contemporary art, rather, it's

the "DEGREE XEROX OF CULTURE," the tran-
scription of everything into visual signs, that has
voided art practice. *The only aim of the image is the
image*, Baudrillard writes. Endlessly solipsistic, an
image can no longer imagine the real because it is
the real.

The depressed antihero of Eldon Garnet's satirical
novel *Reading Brooke Shields* gets picked up by Lisa
and Bob, two earnest Canadian swingers. Once
inside their apartment, he's shown a seat on the
couch. Bob grabs the remote and turns on the
widescreen TV:

*On the screen, a blond woman is sucking a penis.
Moaning. Lisa is leaning back against the screen,
crackling electric static, wrapping her body up against
it. Moaning. Is there no escape from the image?*

For more than a decade, most contemporary art
installations have used video as one of several envi-
ronmental components. But increasingly, "artist's
videotapes," sold to collectors in limited editions,
have become stand-alone works. Museums and
galleries have become venues for works that, two
decades ago, would have been screened as experimental
cinema. (A similar thing has occurred with nonmainstream literature.) The flat monotony of Andrea
Fraser's *Untitled* unfolds on a gallery monitor, but its
polemic-durational quality has much in common
with films made by Danièle Huillet and Jean-Marie
Straub, Guy Debord, and Chantal Akerman. Andrea

Bowers spent months taping readings of the desperate letters sent in the 1960s to the abortion rights activists Patricia Maginnis, Lana Clark Phelan, and Rowena Gurner for her 2005 videotape *Letters to an Army of Three*. With a running time of 55 minutes, the tape is really a documentary film. But it's shown, sold and reviewed as an artwork. A slight shifting of emphasis… there is no longer an audience, no distribution system in place for nonnarrative film, but the impulse to make it and watch it remains, so its affects have migrated into the art world. Consequently, the film becomes less an autonomous act—a thing hurled into the culture—and more like an artifact, a branded product, to be viewed through the career of the artist.

The Bernadette Corporation confronted this fact when they completed their 2003 video-film *Get Rid Of Yourself*. Shot and edited over two years, *Get Rid of Yourself* is a feature-length neo-Godardian interventionist documentary about the 2001 Genoa antiglobalization riots and the widespread frustration with globalization as a fait accompli. The film intercuts mock studio shoots of hyperbolically blank fashion models with hand-held street footage of anarchist youths smashing ATMs and looting supermarkets. Conceived in the 20th century tradition of cinéma vérité, *Get Rid Of Yourself* provides a startling snapshot of somebody's present. Still, BC discovered that the movie was completely unshowable outside the art world. There is no longer a first-degree context for activist film. *Get Rid of Yourself* was, instead, viewed as a work of conceptual art, part of BC's overall project, performed in the shadow of Situationist art, media-fashion, etc. In this sense, part of the film's purpose was negated.

This is very complex, but perhaps in a good way? Conceptual art offers viewers a journey along an associative chain. There is always a bottom. Or rather, the work attains its own life by cannibalizing the half-lives of its sources. Looping back through multiple tropes to arrive at its own existence, the conceptual art work offers itself the protagonist of an old-fashioned, well-crafted story composed through the collision of historical referents rather than characters. Immobilized as we are in the present, it is perhaps more pleasurable to consider the confluence of activism, Situationism, and BC's prior work on the blankness of fashion that occurs in *Get Rid of Yourself* than to ponder the workings of the World Trade Organization.

Outside on the South Loop Chicago street where I'm living this year, students flip open their cell phones and gaze at the tiny rectangular screens as if they were oracles. Cell phones are the most brilliant invention. Youth culture is seized and sold back to itself; you can talk to your friends. At 19, you can no longer expect to have your own room, let alone your own apartment in a metropolitan center, but you can carry your personal space in the palm of your hand. Formed in the late 1990s to investigate forms of blankness, BC adopted their name as a fuck-you to the art world's star system and cultural branding. The ironic fate of their activist film wasn't lost on them.

*The video frame is not a rectangle*, the godfather of structuralist film Hollis Frampton observed less than one decade after Nam June Paik first picked up a Sony video Porta-Pak. *It is a degenerate amoeboid shape passing for a rectangle to accommodate late night TV's cheap programming.* Film, Frampton believed, looks at itself: the frame's radiant rectangle asserts its perimeter. The rectangular edge of the frame marks the boundary between the known and the unknown, the seen and the unseen, what is present and what is completely elsewhere. Looking into the degenerate amoeboid box of the video monitor, Frampton saw "a mandala of feedback." Feedback feeding back on itself... five hundred and twenty-five lines of pixels thrusting and closing. He was the first person to look at video's electronic surface and see a covert circularity, a fabulous orgy of onanism between mind and image. This romance, Frampton feared, was doomed to end badly: the mandala turns into a navel, *a sucking and spitting vortex into which the whole household is drawn.*

Rosalind Krauss describes the terror of this in her 1976 essay *Video: The Aesthetics of Narcissism*. Recalling Nancy Holt's performance in *Boomerang* (1974), a video that Holt produced with Richard Serra, she writes:

*The prison Holt both describes and enacts, from which there is no escape, could be called the prison of a collapsed present, that is, a present time that is completely severed from a sense of its own past. We get some feeling for what it is like to be stuck in that present when Holt at one point says, "I'm throwing things out in the world and they are boomeranging back… boomeranging…. eranging … angining." Through that distracted reverberation of a single word—and even word fragment—there forms an image of what it is like to be totally cut off from history, even, in this case, the immediate history of the sentence one has just spoken. Another word for that history from which Holt feels herself to be disconnected is text.*

Video enacts a collapsed and continuous present, a perpetual motion of things feeding back on themselves. To be smothered by one's own image. Watching Vito Acconci's *Air Time*, Krauss sees the artist skewered on his own image. She likens this state to that of Lacan's analysand, forced to speak into a vacuum of silence until his most heartfelt confessions become no more than air, until all sense of him "self" is thrown into question. For both Frampton and Krauss, the loss of "self" and of "history" was a thing to be feared.

This grim totalitarian prison of self was a far cry from Nam June Paik's delirious vision of a future (our present) when "TV Guide will be as thick as the Manhattan phone book" (*Global Groove*, 1973). Nam June, who'd been an early member of Fluxus, saw the "mandala of feedback" as a gateway to ecstasy:

*My TV is NOT the expression of my personality, but merely PHYSICAL MUSIC, he wrote in 1963. My TV is more than the art and less than the art. I can compose something which lies higher than… or lower than… my personality.*

Perhaps video is not very different from any other art object. Perceptual historiography. The object alone doesn't move us, what matters is what we project onto it. Like the Talmud, all the action lies in the analysis and counteranalysis. But this, too, is old news. Sitting out World War I at the Cabaret Voltaire in Zurich, Hugo Ball, a founder of Dada, read Kant and looked at his shoe polish can and threw up his hands in horror. "Today I saw a shoe polish with the inscription, 'The Thing in Itself.' Why has metaphysics lost so much respect? The citizen nowadays is a commodity, too. For the state."

The college dorm building I live in here in Chicago is managed by Wackenhut Prisons. The tough, middle-aged black female guards in the lobby wear the tight navy blue trousers and shirts of police officers. Each guard wears a shiny aluminum badge with the company logo—a triangular hut, shaped like the dollar-bill pyramid—over her left breast pocket. Wacken-hut. Whacking off in the hut? There's a cheap calendar hung up over the guard desk that shows an American flag superimposed over dreamy American grain fields.

Founded in 1954 by former FBI operative George Wackenhut, the company became a pioneer in the outsourcing of surveillance and terror. Throughout the 1960s, they gathered files on four million suspected American dissidents and went on to open privatized prisons all over the world and six immigrant detention camps in Australia. Tasked with providing untraceable illegal arms for the US military in the 1980s, Wackenhut joined forces with California's Cabazon Indians to build a munitions factory on sovereign Indian land. Weapons produced here were covertly shipped to the Mideast and Nicaragua. In Texas, Wackenhut prisoners build Microsoft circuit boards for $1.25 an hour. Intensely supervised and centrally located, these prison factories compete well with China and India in outsourced computer assembly. In the past seven years, Wackenhut has been summoned to US Federal Court 62 times to face human rights charges brought by present and former prisoners.

I'm not in prison, but in a faculty apartment of a Chicago art institution. When I remark on the

Wackenhut presence, I'm told, "Oh, but these guards have different training."

In 1965 Nam June Paik pointed a new Sony Porta-Pak camera out of a New York taxicab window. He was the first person to purchase and use this equipment, newly launched for the US consumer market. Suddenly everyone could make movies. Within a few years, thousands of hours of videotape had been shot by new, self-trained documentarians. The equipment was awkward and heavy but the process was instant. Because of the extreme difficulty of editing half-inch open reel tape, most of these works were composed by stopping and starting the camera. Video collectives like Raindance, TVTV, and Videofreex produced alternative news shows, street tapes, tapes about childbirth, and alternative soap operas like *The Continuing Story of Carol and Ferd*, a series revolving around the marriage between a porn star and a bisexual junkie.

The aesthetic was process, and for a short time many people truly believed this new technology would transform media culture into an open, interactive democracy. *Alternative media access systems* were being proposed. The proliferation of cable TV channels would present an opening for anticommercial programming to enter mainstream American culture. Or so the collectives believed. What happened was history—a history that would repeated when similar hopes were expressed with the advent of widely available internet—but public access TV (finally put out of its misery by Reagan's deregulation of cable) died a slow death because, given the choice between watching it and CNN, HBO, or MTV, *no one wanted to watch it.* What happened instead was that the visual style pioneered by these early video collectives— jump cuts, hand-held cinema vérité, and real-time documentary—migrated to mainstream TV along with some of its makers. The credits of *Confrontation*, an early HBO reality show in which crime victims confronted their jailed assailants, read like a Who's Who of Global Village and Film/Video Workshop, two long defunct early nonprofits.

I recently rewatched Chris Burden's 1971 videotape, *Shoot*. What makes the work thrilling four decades later is not the smeary black and white lines on the open reel tape, or the act itself, but the willfulness with which it is executed. Chris Burden's friend's off-camera words, *Are you ready?* just barely audible, his tense, *Yes go ahead*—the way his body freezes just before impact. The fractional second before the bullet grazes his arm holds all the drama.

In January I traveled to Puerto Angel, a small Oaxacan beach town that was the scene of my friend, the late David Rattray's story, "The Angel." David and his best friend, Alden Van Buskirk, went there in

1961, a few years after college. They were both 25 and Van was dying of a rare strain of leukemia. Their general plan, as David described it, "was to live there and write books." Forty-five years ago, Puerto Angel might as well have been on the moon. Power lines weren't run out to these towns until the late 1970s. Puerto Angel got its first pay phone two years ago, and it is still shared by four coastal pueblos. In his story, David recalls the flickering light of a kerosene lamp at a beachside café. He imagines himself engraved in a pictorial magazine feature, circa the 1870s. Déjà vu of another century.

"As I pause from writing," David noted, "I can look straight up into the Milky Way. When I climb into the hammock, my feet will point west, towards the Pacific. Van says poetic license is the freedom to do exactly what you feel like doing from one minute to the next."

Time still moves at a different rate in southern Mexico. There are Internet cafes and hotels but the houses behind the main street are still made of palm leaves and wattle. Staying 15 miles north in Mazunte, it took over an hour to reach the payphone in Puerto Angel. First you flag down a taxi truck into the next town, Zippolite; then you wait for the collectivo taxi that won't start its run with less than five passengers.

Two hours inland outside the village of Santa Maria, an American botanist who's building a field research station in the jungle tells me the workers he hired spend 45 minutes to straighten a single bent nail. Living without running water in wattle huts and working for $10 a day, they have all the time in the world. Nails are a rarity.

"The only wars now are not of space, but of time," says the philosopher of speed, Paul Virilio. Last year, the Bill and Melinda Gates Foundation allocated $35 million—money accrued, in some small way, through the labor of Wackenhut prisoners—to purchase mosquito bed nets for 80% of the people of Zambia. Although bed nets have long been acknowledged to be the single most effective means of preventing malaria, no one before this ever addressed the spread of this disease so directly. Simply give nets away. With this and a half dozen other programs, the Gates Foundation has become the world's largest single largest provider of African aid. It's a strangely utopian image, this transfer of capital, i.e., of energy, across the matrix. Stranger still that these funds are derived from the sale of computers, the single most powerful agent in the collapse of space/time at the end of the 20th century. Technology changes the world, and for the better. Technology changes the world into the matrix.

Some of us—mostly those born in 1966, or before—who work in the conceptual echelons of the first world maintain a faint vestigial awareness that life was not always this way. We remember that cigarettes once took the place of cell phones, and if you wanted to reach someone quickly you would not instant message or text but actually *leave your apartment* and knock on their door. We recall an intricate, unwritten protocol surrounding *the visit*, the duration of face-to-face meetings in domestic settings measured out in consumable signifiers: one or two cigarettes, a fresh pot of coffee versus what was left in the pot, a cold drink or a bottle of wine. We have an awareness that the most envied, desirable consumer items—plasma TVs, houses, and cars, all these possessions—are not an end in themselves, or even a trigger to increased consumption. They are the tools of increased mobility, an eternal conduit used to enhance the transaction of business, which—through its constant exchanges of energy—has become more erotic than sex. The most desired plateau is not the stability, the illusion of permanence, once implied by these objects, but perpetual flux. Far more creativity goes into the marketing of products than into the products themselves. Likewise, the fact of the disappeared object is key to conceptual art, a term that is oxymoronic: all art now is conceptual, deriving its value only through context, at a second remove.

The first structuralist film I ever saw was *Chicago Loop* (1976) by James Benning. In it, a stationary camera recorded steam rising out of an industrial chimney for nine minutes. No camera movement, no edits. It was a strange and delirious thrill, the idea that you could sit and watch nothing, a film about nothing. The steam dispersed and striated but the action all took place inside the mind of the viewer.

In the mid-1990s, numerous artists reprised the structuralist aesthetic and ethos to ponder the phenomenological implications of new formal properties inherent to digital video. The question "What does the world look like through a video camera," engaged a new generation of artists. Eager to distance themselves from yesterday's platform of "criticality," they revived essentialist qualities like "beauty" and "the sublime," embracing the fluidity of digital video. The equipment was cheap. The coolness of ambient art defined the look of the work, and the spaces available to show it were massive.

Far better schooled than the original structualists, the next generation devised a rhetoric completely devoid of the wit and DIY charm that marked the work of their predecessors. While the films of Hollis Frampton, James Benning, Ken Jacobs, and Stan Brakhage seemed to speak on some level to the obvious philistine question—*You call this art? Nine minutes of steam?*—with a measure of self-deprecation, the new structuralists were well-armed with critical theory. And of course, by the mid-1990s, the idea that *anyone* outside the art game would be viewing the work was inconceivable.

"Just as the structuralist filmmakers used 'film' in such a way as to reveal a materiality, a shape and a form that characterizes it, so must we be able to make the material 'video' speak of a signal, tape, camcorders, monitors, and projectors," the artist Diana Thater wrote ten years ago. Drawing attention to the elusive materiality of the video medium suddenly seemed to offer a platform from which to engage with much larger questions about the nature of technologized consciousness within the matrix.

"Video," enthused one contemporary, "offers a whole different kind of happiness that has to do with shining surfaces or spinning movement." The "techno-sublime" was hailed by art critics as the decade's most important new genre. Had an old-fashioned philistine wandered into the gallery, he might have mistakenly thought the wall-sized projections of flowers and dolphins were like a Sensurround Nature Channel and not, as one critic put it, "the displacement of narrative onto separate textual systems." For awhile, the liquidity of digital media that thirty years prior delighted Nam June Paik and disturbed critics like Krauss and Frampton, was once again news. As critic Christiane Paul wrote, new structuralist video announced "a paradigm shift in which the artworks cease to embody 'artistic truth' and become 'conditions of possibility,' that is, fluid interactions between manifestations of information."

At the time, Thater argued that by observing video's properties, "we may better use the latent qualities of the medium which, in and of themselves, resonate." But do they? And against what?

Abstracting sheerly physical properties like "fluidity," "displacement," and "dematerialization," the rhetoric surrounding new structuralist video offered no more than the mandala of feedback Frampton saw on the screen thirty-five years ago. "Manifestations of information"? Everyone's stoned. Viewing an installation work of that era in which video footage of an LAPD car chase was projected onto the museum wall, the critic Bruce Hainley wondered at the artist's seeming disinterest in anything beyond colors and pixels. "Vroom fucking vroom," he synopsized.

*In Finitude's Score: Essays for the End of the Millennium*, Avital Ronell considers the videochip implants used to engender memory in *Total Recall* and sees how they co-exist with a condition of stated amnesia. Images come to infuse an amnesiac subject. But these images aren't the same as remembering; rather, they help keep their subjects in a state of eternal amnesia, channel surfing through blank zones of trauma.

"Van's mind is like an all-night movie house," Rattray wrote in "The Angel."

"I sleep, then wake up, the bus standing still. Van tells me there was a couple fucking in the back and the driver and his Cuban assistant joked about the floor show. We just reached the head of the pass. From here on, until we reach the coast tomorrow morning, it's downhill."

Returning to LA after a trip home to visit his family in Lima, the photographer and critic George Porcari observes the framed photographs of Central and Latin American coffee plantations in his local Starbucks and finds them suddenly odd. The images are so generalized they're nearly invisible. In one picture, a dark-skinned man stands in a sea of coffee beans grimacing at the camera. Porcari recalls Sharon Lockhart's photographic series *Teatro Amazonas*— "color photographs of a dark-skinned woman carefully holding various kinds of fruit in her hand. She is self-conscious," he writes, "complicit like the man in the Starbucks picture."

To Porcari, both sets of photographs reference the guilt-wrenching images of third-world death and poverty that came to be known, in the mid-1950s, as "the photography of concern." Yet both sets of pictures, he argues, deliberately situate themselves outside that humanist context, co-opting its visual language and yet sharing none of its intentions or emotional content. Comparing Lockhart's photography with the pictures at Starbucks, Porcari observes: "The two images mirror each other, but as in any mirror everything is reversed. What is 'everything'? Why is one picture in a coffee shop and another in an art gallery? Where is the difference, and how can we find it?"

As the production and marketing of contemporary art becomes indistinguishable from any other corporate transnational venture, it could be that corporations themselves are in the position to change the rules of the game and reclaim the creativity that was once art's domain. After all, the favorite American leisure pursuit outside the home is shopping. It could be argued that entrepreneurial ventures like American Apparel fill the void left by avant-garde process-art projects of the last century, which are no longer practical for artists who must maintain their careers. From its manufacturing philosophy of vertical integration to its marketing and the deliberate location of its gallery-esque stores in urban neighborhoods on the cusp of gentrification, American Apparel resonates against the economic and psychogeographic state of the culture like a gigantic work of conceptual art. As an artwork, it is breathtakingly brilliant in ambition and scope.

"We called ourselves Chia Jen, or The Family," the choreographer Simone Forti wrote of the collective she lived in during the late 1960s. "The life we lived in common provided a matrix for the profuse visions we lived out in various twilights."

Similarly, American Apparel galvanizes the lives of some 5000 employees across the globe. Money, the movement of capital, is just one of its mediums. The company keeps apartments in dozens of cities where employees hang out and take retro-porn pics of each other—the same kind of pics taken and archived by millions of people on Facebook—that will be used in company ads. Business is transacted as flow.

Founder Dov Charney and his colleagues have ingeniously channeled the most loaded social concerns of our time into the "work," which far surpasses the production of t-shirts. At the dawn of the century artists like Bernadette Corporation expressed their generation's disgust with the proliferation of brand. As they wrote in their magazine, "There is nowhere to go or hide or to remain untagged, unlogo'd, undiscovered, unstamped… names and tags will hover over every cosmic labyrinth."

Meanwhile, Dov Charney launched the unbranded t-shirt, creating his own antibrand. While first-world consumers boycotted the outsourced child-labor production of Nike and Gap, Charney rolled out "sweat-shop free" manufacturing in his downtown LA factory. Paying a wage based on fairly-paid piecework, American Apparel at once established itself as a hip antibrand and preempted unionization. If Charney was willing to pay undocumented immigrants $15 an hour in LA, why should they turn to a union, with its Byzantine rules book and dues?

Charney's vertically integrated manufacturing and marketing enterprise has done more to broadcast the obvious cultural links between LA and Mexico City than any municipal government. The plant offers free English classes, and American Apparel billboards across the city urge us to "Legalize LA." Until last year's exhibition at the Hammer Museum, Los Angeles art institutions have remained largely oblivious to the intensely productive art scene in Mexico City. Meanwhile, American Apparel produces a free cultural 'zine from its Mexico City apartment.

The company's merchandising aesthetic includes the display of amateur-produced art that reprises—like much MFA art—reprises various landmarks in conceptual art of the past decades. In the Echo Park store, two series of found archival images—mug shots of women arrested throughout the 1960s by the LAPD, bikini-clad students on Spring Break—evoke work by Mike Kelley, Christian Moeller, and the artists who gathered at Tiny Creatures. In the Hollywood store a surveillance camera aimed on the street feeds images of passers-by back to themselves on a monitor, as in the early video work of Dan Flavin. In an homage to the MFA photographic aesthetic of the late 1990s, the store exhibits a series of large cibachrome prints of car hoods and trees found in interstitial zones of the city.

American Apparel, says its founder Dov Charney, "is a fantasy. It's make-believe. We can do whatever the fuck we want."

"We knew one another, trusted one another's range of possibilities … There was no yardstick to measure individual achievement," Squat Theater collective founder Eva Buchmiller recalled. "We all have our fucking dick in it, it's not just any one person," Charney says of his corporate philosophy. Recruiting talented young women as both content-

advisors and sex partners, Charney creates a paradigm for how life can be lived a different way. Like
Whole Foods, American Apparel polemicizes dreary
consumption: shopping is more than the purchase
of a lettuce or t-shirt; it's an endorsement, a vote for
what the brand means.

Discussing the early videotape *Boomerang*,
Rosalind Krauss glimpsed the power of video art to
"enact a collapsed and continuous present." Three
decades later, this is the default-state of daily life
across the matrix. Information abounds and the
truest dynamic behind movement is commerce.
Using conceptual art's self-reflexivity, it could be that
antibrands like American Apparel, achieving much of
their psychic power from the real-time lives of their
employees, are able to reach more deeply into the
culture than art ever can.

9

## UNTREATED STRANGENESS

*One ought to remember that all cultures impose corrections upon raw reality, changing it from free-floating objects into units of knowledge. The problem is not that conversion takes place. It is perfectly natural for the human mind to resist the assault on it of untreated strangeness; therefore cultures have always been inclined to impose complete transformations on other cultures receiving these other cultures not as they are, but for the benefit of the receiver, as they ought to be.*

— Edward Said, *Orientalism*

1958 Lima—Los Angeles—New York—Los Angeles… 1963 Cuba—Chicago—Los Angeles… 1976 Miami—New York—Miami…

From my notes: A long skinny room in New York, not completely rectangular. Entranceway shaped like a foyer. Floor slopes 6" down on the right. Importation of images (i.e., the space empty or full?) into this room should be neutral. Three-dozen or so prints and photo-collages of varying sizes hung on the walls. A long rectangular table in the main chamber holding numerous digital prints, which can be freely handled. A silver office partition serves as a screen onto which a continuous video loop is projected. A few chairs.

"I'm not a white cube kind of guy. I don't think you can be a white cube guy if you're an immigrant," Jorge Pardo once told Carter Ratcliff.

I've never been to Momenta before, but when George and I sit in his downtown Los Angeles loft discussing how we might install the exhibit in the Williamsburg gallery, an atmosphere gathers: glass-domed railway stations, transient 19th century palaces, magazines, circular banquettes, the Special Collections room of a metropolitan library, the waiting room of a 1920s residential hotel.

My objective in curating this show at Momenta Gallery was to present the work of my friend George Porcari. I've known George since the '90s. For years we've talked about movies and books in the Fogg Library at Art Center College of Art and Design where he works as the Acquisitions Librarian. The library boasts an impressive alumnae: Diana Thater, Mark von Schlegell, Jorge Pardo, Theresa Pendlebury, Steven Hanson, and the late Giovanni Intra have all put in time checking out stuff in the video room and behind the main counter. I'd read Porcari's essays on photography, fiction, and film over the years—essays that, although he's never pursued a career as a critic, consistently probe the patterns of meaning behind the material surface of culture—but I hadn't encountered his visual work until 2006 when Alexis Hall mounted a show of his photos and videotapes at Mandarin Gallery in LA's Chinatown.

That exhibit, entitled *Greetings From LA*, was drawn from two bodies of work: a series of photographs taken around LA between 1976 and 1979, and a subsequent series, taken in Europe during the summer of 2005, some thirty years later. Shot through the windshields of moving cars, his early Los Angeles photos depict dense but bereft slices of urban landscape. Exposed in flat, even light, some of the photos are peopled, some aren't, but all the locations throughout the city feel interstitial.

In *LA Christmas* (1963), sad cones of tinsel planted in striped red and white buckets disappear into Wilshire Boulevard's western horizon against a smogged cyclorama of sky. In *Greetings From LA #9*, a small boy boxed into the back of a moving Dodge station wagon frowns at Porcari's camera, but the left side of his face is angelically bathed in golden-west light. On the other side of the street, a stocky white middle-aged couple gas up their car at an early self-serve 7-11. Caught in this banal moment sometime in the late 1960s, their faces and bodies look oddly regional. And in fact they're only one generation removed from LA's Dustbowl migration of the Great Depression.

Porcari took these pictures during his early 20s. Arrived with his family from Lima less than a decade before, he observed his new home with a feeling of disheartened wonder. Other photographs in this series depict squat office blocks flanked by low-rise commercial storefronts. Space-age novelty food stands sprout from wide asphalt boulevards. Old women and men in powder-blue leisure suits cross streets in Beverly Hills like animals lost from their herd. The images all index typical signs of banality, yet their intention isn't to posit an (equally banal) critique. Rather, they're haunted by sadness… as if Porcari was recording his own sense of displacement, the estrangement of someone who's come from a faraway place and knows he can't return.

Discussing this early work with his friend, the writer Veronica Gonzalez, Porcari remarked:

"When I was very young I was influenced by Cartier-Bresson and Robert Frank … who I still really love, but all that stuff was very much about Cartier-Bresson's decisive moment—catching a particularly poignant moment. But when I saw the films of Nicolas Roeg I realized that if you could stop the frame at any one moment… it would be, first of all, beautiful, but that it would be a kind of nonmoment, nothing would be happening… it would really be nothing. But if could also be so many other things; you could apply your own imagination to everything that came before and came after. It was so rich with possibility and photographers hadn't explored that area."

Traveling in Europe during the summer of 2005, Porcari started to view these foreign cities through the dense mesh of reflections cast by architectural glass. The colors are thick. In *Two Locked Doors*, deep shifting shadows of architectural foliage fill the transparent void of a glass high-rise structure, a corporate cathedral whose lobby looks like a nave. In *Public Phone and Passerby*, blinding postnuclear light radiates from the vanishing point of a street in Paris. The swirls of scratched and painted graffiti on the glass walls of a phone booth are apocalyptically backlit.

There's a great deal of visual information in each of these photographs. For Porcari, the glass surfaces serve as both literal and metaphorical windows onto the disjointed jumble of street. It's as if the subjective sense of displacement he felt as a young man on the streets of Los Angeles has since been institutionalized into the glass-box design of all urban landscape.

I found the show stunning. But it wasn't until he launched his website (www.lightmonkey.net) two years later that I realized how large Porcari's body of work was. Hundreds of images, produced over nearly four decades, most of them documenting his observation of cities in Europe and the US, rural and tourist sites in Peru; the Mexican/USA border and *barrio* neighborhoods in downtown LA.

Porcari modestly describes this work as "photo-journalism," but his ability to capture the transient sweep of global commerce and culture makes it "journalistic" in the largest possible sense. I'm reminded of Magnum Agency founder Werner Bischof (about whom Porcari has written). When Bischoff abandoned surrealism in the wake of the Second World War, he vowed to focus his attention henceforth "on the face of human suffering." He went on to create an astonishing book of images that set out to depict "people and their behavior in the present chaos," but the publication was cancelled because these had already become images no one wanted to see.

*People and their behavior in the present chaos...* Porcari's work sets out to show something like this, but while people often appear in his pictures, they aren't the subject. Deceptively ambient, the photographs are in fact highly composed and intentional. There are no portraits in Porcari's work. Everyone in his world is a bystander. Partly for this reason, his pictures of migrant LA, the Mexican border, and Indian souvenir vendors at Machu Pichu are consistently realistic representations. There's none of the "colorful energy" used as a backdrop for fashion campaigns shot in Morocco or Central America. Porcari sees the third-world as a participant. His photographs neither depict deplorable squalor nor suggest any reason to celebrate the "common humanity" shared by viewers and subjects. In fact, as his numerous series shot all over the world seem to show, there really isn't much difference between the lunchtime crowd outside Time Warner in midtown Manhattan, the tourists gathered at Machu Pichu, or the skinny Latino men in New York sitting on cars beside a Union Square juice cart. Everyone here is a tourist. Porcari's work suggests a world in which the person is no longer defined by any innate singularity, but by his or her place in a state of perpetual flux.

But then again, his photos are also profoundly and classically European. Born a little too late to view French New Wave cinema during the years it was made, Porcari enjoys a romance with the period possible only for someone who's never lived it. His beautiful image, *A Man and a Woman Who Never Met* (for Manuel Álvarez Bravo) evokes the timeless modernist airport of Chris Marker's *La Jetée*. *Peru, Car, Ruins* looks like an incongruous still from Antonioni's *Red Desert*, and isn't the nuclear sun in *Public Phone and Passerby* something like the one that descends at the end of Antonioni's *Eclipse.*

Porcari both indulges and questions this longing for 20th century history in *Aventuras Con Tio César* (1993–2009), his most recent work. The twenty-two prints in the series are all diptychs. The left side of each frame is sourced from "found" family photographs taken by his Uncle César in pre-Fascist Germany. Images from his own 2005 photographs of urban Europe refracted through architectural glass are reproduced on the right. They demonstrate an effect whose cause can be dreamily construed in the mind of the viewer.

Porcari's uncle César left Peru to study medicine in Berlin on a scholarship in the mid-1930s. He traveled by steamship and filled his spare time taking pictures of Berlin's nightlife, streetscape, and parks. More than tourist snaps, less than high art, César's photographs were the work of a 19th or early 20th century *traveler*. Men in dark coats converse for hours at outdoor cafes. A lone deer emerges from the dense silvery foliage of a city park. A woman in a short-sleeved print dress looks at the camera, hands clasped behind her head. When the Nazi Party was elected in 1936, this lost world of Mittel-Europa, and César's stay in Berlin, came to an end. All foreign nationals were ordered to leave. Traveling back to Peru on a packed steamer, César caught TB and died two years later.

I looked at the series with Sylvere Lotringer, a critical theorist born in Europe during the Second World War. Sylvere remarked, "The picture of the deer looks more like a negative than a print. That's why we don't see the reflections. It is a picture without a shadow. The shadows have managed to disappear… like a German romantic story. Even the head of the deer is difficult to see—it blends in with the trees, it looks all mangled. But looking at George's photographs on the right—indirect, shot through glass?—they seem to be in a bubble, as if the present was wrapped up and packaged in cellophane. Untouchable, compared to the past, where you always have a sense of immanence. Or you could say, expectancy. In the past it's as if they're unaware of what is waiting for them, and the waiting itself is part of the picture. The leisure. That's what gives the pictures such a sense of spaciousness and suspense. It's like they're suspended in time, whereas the photographs of the present are suspended in space."

I look at the pictures again. On the left side of *Diptych #10*, a man and a woman stand close together. The black and white photo is cropped. We don't see their heads, just their torsos. He wears a black suit and a tie; she wears a modestly v-necked cardigan jacket. It's a sexy and intimate shot. The way their bodies curve towards each other through the restrained, formal lines of the clothes. On the right side of the frame, a rectangular high-rise reaches into the halated night sky of a city, its glass surface reflecting an off-camera pink light and the yellow halogen lights of the freeway.

Lightness and weight. The awareness of time travel conveyed through all of Porcari's work is compressed in these 22 pictures.

Most critics discussing the work of Jorge Pardo seem compelled to define the aesthetic space, somewhere between architecture, art, and design, that it occupies. Is it a sculpture? Is it a house? Is this even an interesting question to ask? Omitted from these conversations is the intensely social nature of Pardo's work, and the inventive and generous uses to which he puts it. His 2007 installation at MOCA Miami included a full-sized construction called *Mountain Bar*, which is not just the name of a work, but also the name of an actual bar he co-owns in Los Angeles. Mountain Bar (Is it a business? Is it a sculpture?) is an important fixture in the city's artistic community. Since its 2002 opening, Mountain has hosted hundreds of free live events: art talks, music performances, philosophy lectures. Unlike other venues, programming at Mountain Bar is very casual. When UCLA cancelled the Sex Workers Art Show performance the day of the show, Pardo arranged a show at the bar within hours.

A friend of Porcari's since art school, Pardo created three new sculptures for this exhibition that could be used to display George's photographs. Whether designing a house set into a non-graded hill (as he famously did at 4166 Seaview Lane in Mt. Washington) or redesigning the pre-Columbian wing at LACMA, Pardo's work always occurs in response to a site or situation. The sculptures he made for Momenta—*Tables 1 and 2* (2009) and *Partition*

(2009)—were conceived as exhibiting surfaces. Made of highly compressed particleboard, the three pieces were constructed entirely from bisected circles. Deceptively weightless, the tables and screen echo the look of the cheap, throwaway furniture of America's mid-century suburbs. At the same time, they're elegant: the perfectly cut circles evoke the high-modernist look of Miro. Still, they look a little like drink carts or TV tables.

This is the second time Pardo has made sculptural work expressly designed to illuminate the work of other artists. He did this quite literally in his 2001 China Art Objects exhibit with the late Bob Weber, creating lamps used to light Weber's objects. Beyond their utilitarian function—the tables are used to hold prints; the partition is used as a screen to project Naomi Fisher's video—Pardo's high-art revision of cheap furniture gives solid form to the state of perpetual transience revealed by Porcari's photos.


The daughter of a botanist, Naomi Fisher grew up in Miami where she returned from New York to produce thousands of images—paintings, drawing and watercolors, photographs, videotape—depicting young women and dense tropical vegetation. Some of these images are portraits, or still-lives of plants, but mostly her work features athletic and scantily-clad women in jungle environments.

Vines, legs, hair, palm leaves, orchid blossoms and arms. Debuting in New York in the late 1990s, Fisher's exciting, provocative palette inevitably led to her inclusion with the "post-Raphaelite" artists whose large photographs featured demure white female subjects in deciduous meadows. Much has been made by the (male) critics who have viewed Fisher's work of the rampant, psychosexual dynamics that might be discerned in these fecund situations. Is woman's "animal nature" passive? Aggressive? Or, both? There's a lot of blood in her recent images.

Last spring, Fisher rented a rustic cabin in Oleta State Park and invited four dancers to join her for nine days to shoot *Campo Primitivo*. Improvisations arose from their loose routines every day, and she filmed them. The dancer's elegant faces are painted in camouflage. Dresses and hands painted all shades of green like the jungle foliage. Dressed more for a party than a safari, the dancers move freely and of course there's a sexual aspect to this, as there is to all living matter. Collaborating with a group called the Radical Cheerleaders in the late 1990s, Fisher discovered that cheerleading's coy fuck-doll routines could be reshaped into explosions of female energy.

I think Fisher's work is pure heightened play. Girls in the woods, girls in the jungle… who wouldn't want to hang out in there? *Campo Primitivo* is like a wilderness camp where people wake up and act out their dreams in sexier clothing.

# 4. Drift

## 10

## TWELVE WORDS, NINE DAYS

1.
Punta Banda, Baja California North
July 18, 2007

*boredom …*

"I'm very obsessed lately about capitalism and failure," the conceptual artist Stefan Brüggemann remarked to Malcolm McLaren. "How's that?" asked the *eminence grise* of punk nihilism. "Well it's not about criticizing it, but more about just celebrating but then that's very empty, but I kind of get attracted to that," replied Brüggemann.

What struck me about McLaren's part of this dialogue was that he was extremely specific. As if he's spent most of his time since punk's demise acquiring and refining information, i.e., becoming a thinker. It is possible for someone to be highly intelligent, and yet have no information. This condition—usually associated with youth or prolonged adolescence—results often in *boredom*, the existential progenitor of nearly every significant art and cultural movement. I'm thinking dada-surrealism-*dérive*-Guy Debord-East Village punk-mid-'90s grunge/heroin chic-late '90s Los Angeles. Boredom, a brilliant and brazen stupidity, is dazzlingly preemptive. When the bored youth is no longer young, he/she generally either enacts his/her own early demise, or devotes him/herself to acquiring information. Specificity preempts boredom. Like the incandescence of *pop*, boredom cannot be sustained indefinitely. The *seduction* of pop is to render everything nascent, just on the verge of becoming. *No No No NO*, Brüggemann asserts in one of his pieces. Let critics ponder the presence or absence of irony in his use of this two-letter word, is it an homage to Bruce Nauman? In *Obliteration*, Brüggemann's graceful and casual scratches of nothing freeze on the wall as halations. Boredom is pop's weighted corollary, but it can't be sustained once someone acquires an interest in details.

A Brüggeman show entitled *Shallow* featured boxes of Nothing, conjoined with the subtitle of Gilles Deleuze and Félix Guattari's *A Thousand Plateaus* reduced or expanded to giant Styrofoam letters alongside an M&M warehouse in Puerto Rico, *Capitalism and Schizophrenia*… is there another place in the world where this concept would have more and less resonance? *I'll be your mirror.* Taglines of critical thought float in the vacuous space of the gallery, a passive-aggressive performance whose viewers define themselves through their responses.

I think Stefan's real work is to act as a catalyst.


2.
Punta Banda, Baja California North
July 19, 2007


*capitalism …*


Chilly morning, gray coastal fog rolls in across the peninsula. I can't shake this feeling of abandonment, sadness—it's like those years in East Hampton when mornings began with a *weight*. A political scientist from Ottawa, Canada writes about globalization in terms of *extreme loneliness*, and this is a radical thing, to imagine anyone outside the privileged West even having a subjectivity. Contemporary fiction takes this one step further: only upper-middle class domestic life is worth considering. My Grandmother's Cancer, My Divorce, My Subjectivity. And they could be right. The Polish theater director Tadeusz Kantor once staged a play in which a cast of elderly men and women sat at long benches and desks in an old-fashioned primary schoolroom—the modernist nightmare of constant return and repetition.

I CAN'T EXPLAIN
AND
I WON'T EVEN TRY
(Brüggemann—white neon, 2003)

Reinventing society from the inside, the group that
gathered around Havelock Ellis in London during the
late 1880s felt compelled to explain everything. "You
can't build a new wall with old bricks," Ellis wrote, and
they were the bricks: feminist, nudist, socialist, anti-
monogamous, vegetarian, bisexual. They lived alone or
in groups, rarely in couples, pursuing dangerously close
friendships. All had their own work; the women were
childless. They had no preconception of happiness; they
were distrustful of passion. Demolishing most of the
existing taboos around sex, they set out to discover what
sex could actually mean and they found it meant less
than personal confidences. *Skull Fuck, Dirty, Not Dirty,
Tripping Out Through Each Other's Eyes*—they pooled
their pasts and their dreams. They tried to be earnest.

3.
Punta Banda, Baja California North
July 19, 2007

*seduction …*

It's very busy this summer on the peninsula—more
than three times the traffic of last year. The blue and

white bus, "El Micro," is barely an afterthought, used only by drunks and the most destitute. The poor drive Japanese beaters, everyone else drives Lobos and Rams and Expeditions. In less than a year, the land along coastal Highway 1 from Tijuana to Ensenada has been almost completely developed. High-rise condominium towers block the view of the beach, rows of stuccoed townhomes have been dug into the hillside.

The billboards selling these things—now written only in English—all use some form of the word "life" in their copy: *Life Elevated, Oceanview Life, Live your Baja Dream, Endless Moments—A Boutique Coastal Living Experience*. Donald Trump's Baja Tower ad is somewhat more sophisticated, with its genial photo of Donald in a nice business suit: *Trump Baja— Owning here is just the beginning*. The beginning of what? *Capitalism* is the new Catholic church, every-thing turning on death, the threat of mortality so pervasive it's barely a subtext.

This summer I'm studying plot, as if plot might offer escape from the limits of *My Subjectivity*. In the best narrative *movies*, events—or the plot and the pri-mary character(s)—advance seamlessly, locked in a dance, so it's no longer certain which is leading. It's a *seduction*—the same complex formula Jean Baudrillard used (*De la Séduction*, 1979) to describe the metastasized movement of capital. Like Albert Einstein, Baudrillard favored suspense novels.

Georges Perec renounced plot because he feared he had no imagination. It was too much work, making shit up. Still, there was a *motive* behind Perec's formal experiments, a flight both towards and away from telling the story. *Unwriting*, he gives a psychological contour to form and turns the process into the story. *La disparition*, Perec's best known novel, looks conceptual, but since his process is really himself, his books have humor, directness, and warmth absent from most meta-fiction experiments.

(Unwriting this text, I assert my small specificity against conceptual art's grandiose blankness.)


4.
Punta Banda, Baja California North
July 20, 2007


*conflict …*


Last night I felt the spirit that gripped me for months leave my body. I was no longer "in love." I was left with a vivid and heightened sense of the tangible. What was in front of my face—the rooms in this house, the carved rails on the bed, the night wind blowing against the net curtains—became suddenly real, newly interesting. Released, I was happy. Because psychoanalysis (like narrative plot) relies mostly on *conflict*, its structural method cannot account for these hauntings.

5.
Punta Banda, Baja California North
July 21, 2007


*unwriting …*


There's an image of a young man jerking off in a room in front of a mirror. Soft focus. The young man is half-dressed, the colors are muted. It's a very contemporary image. The room is neutral enough. It reeks of nothing but boredom. He's jerking off pretty hard, his face blurred on the dull edge of orgasm.

I make up a story about his life outside of the room. *Nothing* is always a smokescreen. There's always something inside of the box. The boy's name is Derek.

Eight months before taking this photo, Derek was traveling. He grew up in a backwater place (he's Australian) and travel was something he always expected to do because other people had done it before him. He chooses Mexico because it's a cheap third-world place and it's close to America. He's 23, and in a "relationship" with an older artist and this has fucked with his head, and also his plans for the summer. She, Derek's girlfriend (her name is Trina), is on some kind of art fellowship junket in Europe and she was supposed to send him a ticket for the end of the summer when she got settled but so far she hasn't. He doesn't know what he thinks about this, about Trina, except it's making him crazy not knowing what's happening, and also it would be so *nice* to be in Berlin, in Trina's hotel room after living out of a bag and crashing with people for weeks. But the friends-of-friends (actually, friends of Trina's) that he's staying with in LA seem to be pushing him out the door, talking about how *great* it would be to travel alone, how good for his work, et cetera. They introduce him to some 40-year-old rich guy, a painter (Derek's never heard of his work) who goes on and on about his trip there a decade ago, keeping a sketch book.

Finally they drop him downtown at the bus terminal with a *Rough Guide* to Mexico.

Derek catches a Greyhound from LA to the Mexican border. He has no idea where he's going, where he'll sleep, how he'll find a place to sleep, when the bus stops in TJ. The change rate from his country sucks and he resents this. It's not as if he can wire his parents for money, and he's heard nothing from Trina. Also, he doesn't speak Spanish.

Skipping Baja, he catches a bus to Hermosillo, finds a motel for $20 a night, and then starts catching small local buses from town to town, the kind that used to be school buses. Passing through one generic Mexican village after another (goats, dust, diesel, and chickens), Derek considers his future. The thing with Trina seems to be over. Will it hurt his career? Who has she talked to about him? His return ticket back to

Australia is not for another four weeks but he decides to just tough it out because can't figure out what to say to his friends about coming home early.

As he moves farther south, he starts finding youth hostels, not that he meets anyone interesting but at least they're cheap and they give him some destination. But then his money gets stolen and he calls up his friend Gilbert in Melbourne practically weeping and Gilbert wires him $400. Somehow this calms him down, and he decides to spend the rest of his time at the beach in southern Oaxaca. One of Trina's friends gave him a book about two guys who went down to Puerto Angel in the early '60s and ended up taking hallucinogens with an evil police commander.

In Puerto Angel, he finds a cheap Casa de Cuartos and there are other foreigners there, other travelers. He settles into a pleasant routine of swimming and sunbathing during the day, and moving between four or five local bars in the evening. On his fifth day he's lying out at Playa del Panteón. The beach is pretty empty at mid-afternoon. There's just one other guy snorkeling out by the rock jetty. The locals are OK about sunbathing nude on this beach, and Derek sits up on his towel watching the waves. While he's sitting, the snorkeler starts moving around fast in the water, not snorkeling at all, but swimming against a rip-tide that's pulling him out of the bay. The guy ripped off his mask and Derek runs out on the jetty.

The guy is flapping around by this point. Derek's still naked from sunbathing and he crouches at the end of the rocks and he doesn't know what to do, he's not much of a swimmer, and the guy is looking directly at him. For the first time all summer Derek has no thoughts at all. Finally, the guy's head disappears under water.

Holy shit. Derek walks back to the beach and puts on his cut-offs. There's no way he can go back to sunbathing. The drowning has ruined the afternoon's drowsy calm. Derek tells no one what happened. He goes back to his room and packs up his things. The next morning he catches a bus to Mexico City and changes his ticket to go back to Australia.

6.
Punta Banda, Baja California North
July 22 2007


*looks conceptual … misunderstanding*


Brüggemann talks in an interview about concepts arrived at while traveling. *Does he maintain a studio,* he's asked. Yes, but (no surprise, he's an international contemporary artist) he spends most of his time on the move. So he adapts, turns his laptop computer into a portable hermitage, a locus of concentration that can be entered wherever he physically finds himself. In the late '80s, the musician Fred Frith foresaw a future in which culture would be made exclusively by individuals able to function as *small intelligent mobile units.* What's in your PowerBook? Travel, the condition of being nowhere and everywhere, makes the work very open, contemporary. It *looks conceptual,* wrought in the crepuscular dawn of endless transience.

The poetics of marketing: since everything is available, the point is no longer to *have* things but to use them as stations in eternal flux, leveraging into the infinite. *Trump Baja: Owning here is just the beginning.* Far more creativity goes into the marketing of products than into the products themselves. Likewise, the fact of the disappeared object is key to conceptual art, a term that (like "capitalism") is oxymoronic: *all* art now is conceptual, deriving its value only through context, at a second remove.

Or am I *misunderstanding*?

7.
Punta Banda, Baja California North
July 23, 2007


*critique … pop*


Christy arrived last night from LA. We drove up to Maneadero this afternoon and went to the park. The park sits just two streets behind the national highway, but everything's different—there's a wrought-iron gazebo, old benches, tall eucalyptus. A man rides up on a horse. The late afternoon light is golden and soft. Christy takes photos.

I'm reading *Spook Country*, William Gibson's new novel. Hubertus Bigend (an evil cross between Malcolm McLaren, Jean Baudrillard, and Charles Saatchi) tells Hollis, the androgynous heroine, "The *pop* star was actually an artifact of preubiquitous media." Bigend is clearly the bad guy, but the book is a smooth string of pop product placements for boutique hotels and "cool" merchandise. Reflecting the brushed aluminum surface of ambient life, a narcissistic *critique* of the present.

8.
Punta Banda, Baja California North
July 24, 2007

*political … movie*

ALL MY IDEAS ARE IMPORTED
ALL MY PRODUCTS ARE EXPORTED
(ALL MY EXPLANATIONS ARE RUBBISH)
—Stefan Brüggemann, *Social Sculpture* 2007

There is a recurring belief that certain decisions were made for us while we were still lost in the womb of our childhoods. Transactions were brokered in windowless rooms. Armies of people speaking in bland West Coast American accents. Always, the real story was elsewhere. Las Vegas, Nevada. Phoenix and Tempe. What were the voices describing? A carton of water-stained books found in an old man's garage. Proliferation of data surpassed proliferation of nuclear warheads. Old metal, junked electronics. Dictation equipment. Deposing as testament. The sloppiness of all this. *Political* porn.

There is a recurring belief that to locate this, this margin of error, would be to trace a historiography of one's present amnesia. Can no longer remember the *movie* where the person was part of the process. Hallways leading to multiple doors. Behind them, a basketball court, loudspeakers, coaxial wires. Folding tables and chairs. Conversion. Set theories, in which the system eventually takes over. Each door leads to the room.

9.
Punta Banda, Baja California North
July 25, 2007

*blind*

Two years ago when my vision dropped off, I met someone who wanted to kill me. I was already half *blind…* Death had drawn me a few times before, but I always invented something to do. Running and stumbling. *Pussy smokes a cigarette, pussy blows smoke—penis exfoliation shaved pussy stories Michael*

*Wertheim penis extraction Michael Wertheim litigation mediacom pretty women with cocks worldcast net Albany sex protein diets property management lingerie sale...* the search-engine log of a website based in Romania. When I researched my killer online I felt like something was looking over my shoulder, a primitive counting machine buried inside the circuit board. And this turned out to be true.

## 11

## THE FAILED COLLECTIVE

(For the Extra Room: Adam & Mara)

There's no such thing as a *failed* utopian community; or, if the collective is an experiment in shared time, how can time fail? A great sense of failure couches every success. YES and SO WHAT? Is That All There Is To It? What goal do you imply with the phrase, "failed collective?" Utopia—static and therefore unreal—is never the point. Collectivity arranges itself around a desire for something, to produce something, to become something else (and who cares what else?) beyond its individual members.

Back in Auckland last month, Ann Shelton and Gilbert took me to Piha, the still-remote collection of beach shacks protected by hills 45 minutes out of the city, to show me the place where Giovanni was buried. Well not really buried, his body was cremated, but still. We parked in the small dirt lot near Piha's wide sandy beach and walked up a hill for 15 or 20 minutes. In the elbow of one of the switchbacks, we stopped. Gilbert and Ann showed me the break in the bush where the bleary procession came to a halt and someone (Was it Gilbert? He was G.'s closest friend but he is not in the art world. It might have been someone more famous.) uncorked the ashes. The idea was to scatter them into the ocean, but it's a dizzying drop, at least 400 feet to the bay, so at first the cremains landed on gorse bushes.

More than 200 people attended the funeral and it lasted three days because that's how much time the indigenous Maoris allot for ritual mourning. The death brought all these people together and everyone was themselves: the drunk and the timid, the loud-mouths, the tormented girls, the grandiose artists. Ann, who's in her 40s, told me the funeral party got out of hand. After 24 hours, she wanted to scream, Haven't We All Had Enough?! Still, everyone needed to gather and spin through predictable cycles of grief, the public the private, what shouldn't be seen and what's best forgotten.

It's been more than a year since that happened and now the grave is a nice place to visit. I envy G.'s grave. After all of his travels he rests in a beautiful place just a short drive from downtown, where generations of artists have liked to ditch work for the day and get high and picnic. (Down below in the bay, a flotilla of merchant ships wrecked in another century.)

Still all of that action—the drinking the drugs the confessions the confrontations—had to play out against the electric green field at the base of the hill before there could be this powerful silence. G.'s death imparting that silence. He was ambitious at times pompous but mostly generous, and he died on the brink of attaining enough power to conclude that power, once attained, can be pretty boring. That stupid play we used to act out at school, August Strindberg's *The Stronger*. Which woman, the wife or the mistress, will annihilate who? Does abjection trump cunning? Who cares? G.'s death, like his life, was a great gift to his friends and also iconic, the way he liked things to be. His death, the death of everyone's youth, that's what was grieved, and what happens next will always be boring. The group disperses… "real life," the real anticlimax.

Of course the ashes are no longer here. Wind carried them from the gorse and the waves took them away.

ACKNOWLEDGMENTS

Grateful acknowledgment to Creative Capital/ Warhol Foundation for their support of work on "You Are Invited To Be The Last Tiny Creature," and to my editor, Hedi El Kholti who suggested the topic.

Thanks also to Matt Fishbeck, Paul Gellman, Jason Yates, Rachel Detroit, Geneva Jacuzzi, Marco Vera and especially Janet Kim for their willingness to think back to that time and discuss it. Julianne Pierce commissioned "Indelible Video" for the Adelaide Festival. I'm grateful for her support and for the ongoing dialogue I've enjoyed with Moyra Davey, George Porcari, Marc Lowenthal, Sylvère Lotringer, Hedi El Kholti, and Jim Fletcher, John Kelsey, Anton Walczak and Bernadette Van-Huy of The Bernadette Corporation. I'd also like to thank Philip Valdez for his support and belief in this project.

# semiotext(e) intervention series